The Placebo Response and the Power of Unconscious Healing

The Placebo Response and the Power of Unconscious Healing

Richard Kradin

Routledge
Taylor & Francis Group
New York   London

Routledge is an imprint of the
Taylor & Francis Group, an informa business

Routledge
Taylor & Francis Group
711 Third Avenue,
New York, NY 10017

Routledge
Taylor & Francis Group
2 Park Square,
Milton Park, Abingdon,
Oxfordshire OX14 4RN

First issued in paperback 2014

Routledge is an imprint of the Taylor and Francis Group, an informa business

© 2008 by Taylor & Francis Group, LLC

ISBN 978-0-415-95618-5 (hbk)
ISBN 978-1-138-88168-6 (pbk)

Visit the Taylor & Francis Web site at
http://www.taylorandfrancis.com

and the Routledge Web site at
http://www.routledge.com

I dedicate this book to my wife, Karen,

and to my children

Rachel, Sarah, Ben, Mike,

and to Daniel and Michael,

for being patient with me while

I was preoccupied with this project. Although

they have never quite understood what exactly it

is that I do as a profession, they can rest assured

that they are not alone in their confusion.

Contents

Acknowledgments

This text has been several years in the making. The inspiration for it arose out of my musings concerning how the mind and body interact in health and disease. The idea of developing an explanatory model for the placebo response was motivated by a National Institutes of Health grant application that I prepared several years ago. Aspects of this model have previously been presented in journal publications (Kradin, 2004a, 2004b), but they have matured into what is presented here. I am grateful to my colleagues for encouraging me to write this text, in particular to Robert Bosnak, who has devoted his career to mind–body interactions. I thank my editors at Routledge for recognizing the importance of this topic. My thanks to Michelle Forrestall Lee for her expert assistance with the artwork and to Linda Arini for helping to compile the manuscript. Finally, Joe, the incorrigible dachshund, and Simon, the doe-eyed Rhodesian ridgeback, were my constant companions during this project.

Introduction

Despite its ancient origins, medicine is a young science. The substantial progress made over the last several centuries has barely scratched the surface of how the body functions in health and disease. It is important to recognize this and not to become too self-satisfied with the current state of medical science.

Several years ago, while serving as the research director of the Mind/Body Medical Institute of Harvard Medical School, I was asked to develop a research program aimed at elucidating the mechanism of the placebo response, which is the cause of beneficial effects seen in response to a non-specific treatment.

The scientific literature includes deep disagreements concerning the placebo response. Although many practicing physicians hold that it is a critical aspect of therapeutics, a sizable number claim that placebo effects are simply imaginary. Almost nothing is known concerning how placebos yield their effects.

Coming to grips with the placebo response has not been a simple undertaking. It has required a reexamination of virtually everything that I had previously taken for granted with respect to medical therapeutics. For most of my career, I paid little attention to the placebo response. In medical school, I was taught that placebos were sugar pills administered to patients in past eras. When later in my career I designed and conducted clinical trials, I recognized that placebo effects could confound the interpretation of therapeutic results. That was the extent of my knowledge, and I suspect that it was comparable to that of most of my colleagues.

Despite limited interest in the topic, my unusually broad training had prepared me to investigate the placebo response. I have completed formal training in internal medicine, pathology, and psychoanalysis, and have endeavored with some success to contribute to all of these disciplines. My multidisciplinary interests have provided a deep appreciation of the complexities and nuances of disease and therapeutics.

From my perspective, the field of medicine has seemed comparable to the parable of the blind men and the elephant, in which each man gropes the immense subject but can appreciate only a piece of it. Physicians are often highly specialized in their areas, and, while generally prepared to address questions in their areas of expertise, they often ignore those areas in which they are less proficient. The interface between two fields is particularly susceptible to being overlooked, and this is especially true of mind–body processes such as the placebo response.

With an increasing appreciation of the importance of the placebo response, I grew perplexed as to why one of the most important topics in medicine has for centuries been systematically neglected. It is currently my opinion that the substantial ambiguities that inhere to medical therapeutics will never be resolved until the placebo response has been vigorously addressed.

However, few physicians or medical scientists are authoritatively prepared to address the complexities of the placebo response. My research required a consideration of medical history, mythology, psychology, philosophy, ethics, cognitive science, neurobiology, and immunology. Disturbing doubts arose concerning how medical research is currently being conducted and supported. At times, the bedrock of medical therapeutics appeared to represent a bed of quicksand.

Consequently, this text is primarily devoted to the placebo response, while it also a critical commentary on medical science and how medicine is currently practiced. The reader is forewarned that this treatise will not mainly extol the "amazing power" of the placebo response. I was once approached with the proposal of writing such a text but quickly declined the offer. I chose instead to write a sober critique of what we currently know and do not know about the placebo response and medical therapeutics.

Some of the material in this text appears in other texts on this topic as well. This was, unfortunately, unavoidable, because the field is small and has inspired a limited literature. However, I have purposely chosen to pare the redundant material down and to convey what I believe to be the major issues that surround the placebo controversy rather than to fill this text with numerous examples of placebo effects. Readers who wish to examine those in more detail can find them appropriately referenced in this text.

A large section of this book is devoted to an explication of mind–body physiology and to the putative pathways of the placebo response. Much of this discussion is based on recent findings in developmental neurology and psychology that have attempted to elucidate what occurs in the mind–brain during early infantile attachment. A major thesis to be presented here is that the placebo response develops in parallel to these events. This idea, I trust, will be argued convicingly.

The question of how a unitary placebo response might be responsible for a wide diversity of placebo effects has exercised my thoughts for quite some time. It is my belief that phenomena of extensive complexity such as the placebo response cannot be addressed adequately by the linear methods of medical science but instead require other existing scientific approaches.

I hope to convince the reader that the placebo response is an innate salutary mind–body activity that has contributed to the continuing success of *Homo sapiens* as a species, and that it is evidence of our mutual interdependence. This text is a polemic aimed at raising the consciousness of both the lay reader and my medical colleagues by arguing the importance of coming to grips with the placebo response rather than ignoring or deprecating it.

1 The Placebo Response

Mind Over Matter or a Matter of Perspective?

Who shall decide when doctors disagree?

Alexander Pope

Introduction

Can the mind promote healing of the body? What is the placebo response, and how does it contribute to therapeutic efficacy? Is there one placebo response or many? If you are presently reading this book, chances are that you are interested in these questions. But, definitive answers have continued to evade scientists, and you may be surprised to learn that they remain controversial. Let us begin by examining some of the varied viewpoints concerning the placebo response.

In a recent report Dr. Andrew Leuchther, professor of psychiatry at the University of California, Los Angeles, reported on

Table 1.1   Perspectives on the Placebo Response

Historical basis of all prescientific medical therapeutics
Nonspecific intervention designed to placate patient's complaints
Confounding factor in therapeutic interventions
Imaginary element in the deluded minds of doctors and patients
Unaddressed factor in the philosophy of medical science
Anomalous scientific phenomenon
Complex mind–body response that is the basis of endogenous healing

the results of imaging the brains of patients with major depression (Patterson, 2002). Some of these patients had developed positive therapeutic responses, but not to an antidepressant—to a placebo. According to Leuchther, "We were just looking at the placebo group as a control group. It was really quite a surprise to us when we ... could see that they had significant changes in brain function" (ibid. p. 1).

What Leuchter and his research team discovered was that the brains of the placebo responders showed changes in activity comparable to those of patients who had received antidepressant medication for several weeks. Placebo had produced therapeutic effects and changed brain activities in ways that were indistinguishable from antidepressant medication. Yet Leuchter's remarks convey the surprise that physicians often express concerning the ability of a placebo to produce objective changes in the body's physiology. From their perspective, placebo effects are either imaginal, or frankly fictitious, and they are incapable of leaving footprints in the material world.

The reader may also be surprised to learn that placebos come in various forms and are not only pills. Both surgical procedures and other therapeutic interventions can also be placebos. In fact, placebo effects have been reported in any situation in which an offer to treat has been made. But from another perspective, placebo effects are not primarily the source of salutary effects, rather they confound what was thought to be specific therapies. Consider the study of Moseley et al. (2002), in which a widely performed arthroscopic surgical procedure for the treatment of osteoarthritis was critically evaluated. Arthroscopy allows inspection of a joint cavity via an illuminated fiberoptic scope. In this procedure, the skin overlying the joint is anesthetized, and an incision is made, via which the arthroscope is introduced. With the arthroscope, it is possible to remove the fragments of degenerated cartilage that are thought to be causing inflammation, pain, and loss of joint function.

Prior to this study, arthroscopic knee surgery was considered standard practice, and nearly three-quarters of a million arthroscopic surgeries were performed annually. However, in this clinical trial, while one group of patients underwent arthroscopic joint surgery, another group was anesthetized and given three stab wounds to the skin with a scalpel—but no cartilage fragments were removed. Researchers refer to this as *sham surgery*. It is designed to control for the nontherapeutic aspects of a surgical procedure and to purposefully mislead subjects into believing that their surgery was completed. Yet both groups showed comparable levels of improvement with respect to their knee pain following their surgeries. The researchers concluded that if arthroscopic surgery was no better than sham surgery, then "the billions of dollars spent on such procedures annually might be put to better use" (Mosely 2002, p. 88).

How can an eminently rational therapeutic approach be no more effective than a sham treatment? Philosophers of science have long recognized that rational ideas do not necessarily constitute scientific proof; unfortunately, many doctors continue to ignore this fact. Too often, they base their conclusions on inference rather than on direct observation. Studies like this one are important, as they raise questions with regard to the practices that are taken for granted.

The role of the placebo response in this study was that of a "spoiler." There was little consideration as to why sham surgery was effective, although it clearly was, as both groups showed a 50% persistent improvement in their symptoms. The aim of the study was limited to determining whether the test procedure was superior to placebo; explaining the findings was of little interest.

Despite numerous studies like these that appear to offer convincing evidence for the potency of placebo responses, some skeptics continue to doubt their efficacy. Consider a recent study by Hrobjartsson and Goetzsche (2001), Danish epidemiologists at the University of Copenhagen. They conducted a meta-analysis of 114 previously published clinical trial in which subjects had received placebos, or no treatment, as controls. Meta-analysis is a statistical approach that probes data from previously reported studies. It can be helpful in determining whether a treatment is actually effective, when the results from multiple studies are ambiguous.

The trials analyzed by Hrobjartsson and Goetzsche (2001) included the administration of pills, physical manipulations, and psychological interventions. They divided these trials into those yielding binary (i.e., yes or no) responses and those with continuous outcomes, i.e., including a range of values that could be analyzed quantitatively. The results demonstrated that placebos did improve subjective outcomes, whereas objective outcomes were generally unaffected. Hrobjartsson and Goetzsche concluded that there was "little evidence that placebos in general have powerful clinical effects" (p. 1607).

In an editorial response to this report, John Bailar (2001), a Harvard public health physician, acknowledged these findings but concluded, "There is a pesky utterly unscientific feeling that some things [placebo responses] just ought to be true" (p. 1632). He hastened to add that few clinicians would be willing to abandon what they believed to be an effective and innocuous means of alleviating patient discomfort. The latter sentiment is underscored by Eric Cassells (2004), an academic physician:

> I would happily give up the use of (say) calcium channel blockers,
> as important as they have been in the treatment of heart disease, if I
> could be assured a similar mastery of the placebo effect; it would be
> useful in more patients. One would think that something as potent as

the placebo effect would have been subject to at least as much study as most pharmaceuticals, but that is unfortunately not the case (p. 113).

Can Cassells' (2004) sentiments be reconciled with the findings of Hrobjartsson and Goetzsche (2001)? In letters to the editor in response to the article by Hrobjartsson and Goetzsche, Lilford and Braunholtz (2001), scientists at the University of Birmingham in the United Kingdom, argued that in a clinical trial with a placebo control, there is a 50–50 chance patients will receive placebo rather than active treatment, whereas patients who receive placebos in noncontrolled medical practice expect an active intervention 100% of the time. They proposed, "If subjects do not believe that they received the active treatment, no placebo response is expected, which is what Hrobjartsson and Goetzsche found" (p. 163). Doubt, these researchers insisted, has a strong negative influence on the potency of placebo responses.

The conduct of clinical trials, as the Birmingham scientists contend, may truly be at odds with the factors that promote placebo effects. However, this explanation, at least by current standards, is not scientific, even if correct. Whereas clinicians may believe that potent placebo effects occur in practice, can they prove it? Medical science requires empirical observation and controlled experimentation. But what is to be done when the scientific method itself interferes with the subject being investigated?

From this perspective, the placebo response assumes yet another role—that of a potential scientific anomaly—for which the prevailing scientific methods cannot be applied. When this is the case, one may apply a new mode of experimentation that can hopefully adequately describe the phenomenon of interest. Alternatively, an entirely new scientific approach may be necessary. Anomalies are often responsible for entire paradigm shifts in science.

One might also conclude that there is no incontrovertible evidence that the placebo response exists, in which case this text ends here. The fact is that there actually is no completely convincing evidence for placebo effects and that it is virtually always possible to find alternative explanations for them. But that is to hold the placebo response to a higher standard than other elements of medical science. In addition, as philosopher of science Karl Popper (1972) opined, it is only the deniability of an explanatory model that disqualifies. Currently, no one has been able to prove that placebo effects do not exist, so thankfully there will be more to say about them.

Cause and Effect?

The fact that placebo effects are not separable from other therapeutic effects presents a serious challenge to medical science. We are inclined to think that medical interventions *cause* therapeutic effects, but this view may be too simple. Most of us rarely ponder what is meant by *causality*. But 18th-century philosopher David Hume (1888; Figure 1.1) did. He insisted that all scientific observations be grounded in experience rather than in

Figure 1.1   David Hume. Hume was one of the great Scottish philosophers of the Enlightenment. His views on empiricism and causality had a great impact on the philosophy of science in the West.

abstraction. Hume was a radical empiricist. When he addressed the question of causality, his conclusions were unsettling. To understand his reasoning, consider the following two examples. First, a white billiard ball hits a red billiard ball, and the red billiard ball moves. Second, you are walking down a highway and discover an automobile crushed against a tree; its windshield is broken, and there is a man inside the car who is unresponsive. A dog walks by and pays little attention to what has occurred.

The proximity of events in space and time is often the compelling argument for causality. The white ball hits the red one, the red one moves; Q.E.D. As for the other scene, here no action has actually been observed, yet causality is still inferred. However, the dog, whose mind may not be comparably inclined to view events as causal—at least not for the situation that has been described—infers nothing. Rather, it sees only what is there (i.e., a car, a tree, and a man); that's all.

In Hume's (1888) opinion, in neither example is the observer justified in attributing causality to the events. He argued, rather, that all of these events are separate. Whereas, the red ball does move when struck by the white one, did anyone observe a *cause*, or is one being inferred? But what does this have to do with placebo effects or, for that matter, with any therapeutic effect?

Consider the following. Suppose a patient receives a drug for a set of symptoms. The next day, he is better. What caused the improvement? The answer is that we do not know because we were unable to observe what transpired. But in practice, doctors and patients both often attribute causes for changes in medical conditions with little proof other than the proximity of an intervention. According to Hume (1888), scientists must recognize how the mind tends to create explanations like causality and not be enticed by them.

As will become increasingly evident, only when therapeutic interventions are strictly controlled can they be judged effective; cause and effect can rarely be established. This perspective was encountered in the sham surgery trial. The only question that could be answered was whether arthroscopic surgery was better than placebo. It was not possible to conclude that either arthroscopic surgery or sham surgery caused the beneficial effects that were observed.

In practice, few therapies are subjected to sufficient rigor to determine whether they are even effective. As a consequence, many eventually prove to be placebos. While this does not diminish the importance of placebo effects, it does caution that medical science must take care to distinguish between what human nature and human ingenuity each bring to the realm of therapeutic success. Only in recent times has there been any recognition that treatment effects might be attributable to multiple sources; before, there simply was no conception of placebo effects. The progress of medical therapeutics has largely been due to the increasing discernment of how placebo effects contribute to treatment. But, to clarify what placebo effects are, it is first necessary to explore the nature of disease and healing.

2 The Basis of the Placebo Response in Sickness and Healing

All is flux; nothing stays still.

Diogenes

Healing and Placebo

It is impossible to know what first motivated man to care for the sick by augmenting the healing processes of nature. Healing is not unique to man; it is seen in all forms of life. Extraordinary healings occur regularly in other species. Reptiles and amphibians can spontaneously regenerate entire limbs, without ever consulting a physician. Snakes shed their old skins and develop new ones in a process of biological renewal. Man was undoubtedly curious and wished to benefit from the knowledge of how these processes occurred. The caduceus, a wooden staff entwined by two snakes, was one of the earliest symbols of medical therapeutics, symbolizing man's regard for the achievements of nature.

Although man does not possess the extraordinary healing capacities of reptiles, he does exhibit a wide variety of restorative processes that operate in the service of health, including the cellular repair of genetic mutations, the elimination of infectious agents, and the destruction of incipient neoplasia by immune mechanisms. These activities are both highly efficient and automatic, which is why we rarely require medical attention. However, with the passage of time, these processes begin to fail, accounting for the increased incidence of disease in old age.

The placebo response is a mode of self healing that is evoked by the social transactions of the therapeutic encounter. Those who design clinical trials refer to this as a response to the *offer to treat*, but it is more than that. Unfortunately the term *placebo response* conveys nothing about its mode of action. Later in this text, an explanatory definition of the placebo response will be offered, but for now the following definition may suffice. Norman Cousins (1995), a writer who spontaneously recovered from an incurable disease, said the following about placebos:

> The placebo is not so much a pill but a process. The process begins with the patient's confidence in the doctor and extends through to the whole functioning of his own immunological and healing system. The process works not because of any magic in the tablet but because the human body is its own best apothecary and because the most successful prescriptions are filled by the body itself (p. 63).

Disease and Healing

To position the placebo response properly within the field of therapeutics, it is necessary to explore how it relates to disease and healing. The elements that conribute to healing have been selected by nature for their adaptive benefits, as those organisms that can heal themselves effectively in response to injury or disease are more likely to survive long enough to transmit their genes to the subsequent generation (Nesse & Williams, 1996).

However, the economy of nature is such that adaptive changes are rarely novel; rather, they arise from activities that may previously have served very different purposes. For example, macrophages—white blood cells that play an important role in scavenging microbes and in amplifying immune responses in man—have evolved from a primitive cellular element of clot formation in prevertebrates.

Nature is Janus-faced; the same factors that contribute to healing also contribute to disease. Consider tuberculosis, a disease caused by an ancient soil bacterium, *Mycobacterium tuberculosis*. Infectious disease is a contest that pits the capacities of the host against those of the infective agent. In the case of *M. tuberculosis*, the organism has developed certain virulence factors that make it almost impossible for the host to eradicate it. Instead, the host's immune system attempts to contain the organism within scavenging macrophages and then walls it off with scar tissue. When someone goes for a tuberculosis skin test, what is being evaluated is whether there may be small numbers of potentially viable mycobacteria lying dormant somewhere in the body.

In most cases, the host response is sufficient to limit the spread of the mycobacteria, which continue to survive enveloped in an immune cocoon. But in some individuals with decreased immunity due to advanced age, steroids, pregnancy, chronic disease, or human-immune deficiency virus (HIV) infection, the mycobacteria either continue to grow following the initial infection or are reactivated at some later point. The disease that we call tuberculosis results from the composite changes induced by both the mycobacteria and the host inflammatory response to the infection.

Immune white cells produce cytokines: small, molecular-weight proteins that amplify the immune response but that also produce fever, malaise, and anorexia. All of these responses are potentially adaptive, as they effectively inhibit the reproduction of the mycobacteria. The beneficial effects of fever were demonstrated in a study published by Doran et al. (1989) in the *Journal of Pediatrics* in which febrile children with chicken pox received either acetaminophen, a common antipyretic used to lower body temperature, or a placebo. The children who received placebo reported less nasal stuffiness and showed higher antibody levels, indicating the potentially positive effects of fever on immunity.

But in tuberculosis, cytokines also produce the night sweats and progressive wasting that was once termed *consumption*. When patients succumb to tuberculosis, it is as much the result of their own immune response as the virulence of the organism.

Sickness Behavior

Scientists have coined the term *sickness behavior* to denote the malaise, weakness, fatigue, and anorexia that characterize illness. Sickness behavior is due to the activities of cytokines, including interleukin-1 (IL-1), tumor necrosis factor (TNF), and IL-6—the same molecules that caused the symptoms and signs encountered in tuberculosis (Dantzer et al., 1998). But cytokine production is not limited to the immune system. They are also synthesized and released by cells of the nervous system during inflammation. Cytokines circulate and participate in molecular cross-talk between the immune and nervous system, effectively yielding a supersystem of psycho-neuro-endocrine-immune activities that mediate mind–body interactions in disease. In addition, the autonomic nervous system can directly influence the activities of immune cells during sickness, as psychoneuro-immunologists Steven Maier and Linda Watkins have (1998) demonstrated.

When purified inflammatory cytokines are injected into healthy animals, including man, the response is characteristic (Watkins, 1995). The subject withdraws from his surroundings and develops fever, malaise, and anorexia: the stereotypic features of sickness. But sickness is not just physiological dysfunction; it is also a nonverbal behavior that communicates to others that something is wrong. Social animals are attuned to when a member of their kind is sick. Indeed, astute health professionals pride themselves in being able to recognize the earliest subtle cues of sickness in patients.

Anthropologists have noted that sickness behavior elicits one of two responses: concerned attention or aversive avoidance. These responses are likely rooted in mammalian behavior. Young mammals are regularly cared for by adult members of the group, and even cross-species concern for the young has occasionally been observed. This may have inspired ancient mythic motifs, for example, that of Romulus and Remus, the legendary founders of Rome, who, it was claimed, were raised by wolves.

Which response will be observed is unpredictable. From a Darwinian perspective, altruistic behavior serves the aims of evolution when directed at close relatives who share genes in common (Dawkins, 1990). But exceptions are well recognized and this prompted philosopher Arthur Schopenhauer (1995) to consider what factors might be operating when an individual risks his or her life to save that of an unrelated individual.* Altruistic behavior is generally valued within civilized society, and it is the idealized goal of caring professions. In *When Elephants Weep*, Masson and McCarthy (1995) examined the concerned behavior

---

* However, the amount of genetic information shared by all members of a species and even between species makes this standard argument somewhat specious.

of primates and offered the following anecdote of how a gorilla in captivity responded to a sick research scientist:

> A woman who was working with Koko, the signing gorilla, had indigestion one day and asked Koko what she should do for a "sick stomach." Koko, who was given extra orange juice whenever he was ill, signed, "stomach you orange." The woman drank some juice, told Koko she felt better, and offered her some juice…. Ten days later, when the same woman visited again and gave Koko some juice, Koko offered it to her and had to be reassured that the visitor felt fine, before she would drink the juice herself (p. 37).

Sir William Osler (Figure 2.1), a founder of the Johns Hopkins Hospital, suggested that "medicine arose out of the primal sympathy of man with man; out of the desire to help those in sorrow, need, and sickness" (Osler, 1921 p. 6). But most primates are, in fact, dispassionate and tend to ignore the sufferings of their own kind. Jane Goodall's (1995) field studies with chimpanzees demonstrated that monkeys rarely exhibit caretaking behavior in the wild, where most seriously ill members of the group are abandoned. Ambivalent responses to illness have also been documented in human societies, in which, according to medical historian Roy Porter (1997):

> The sick person is treated as a child, fed, and protected during illness or incapacity … [or] sufferers leave the group, or as with lepers in medieval Europe, [they are] ritually expelled, becoming culturally dead before they are biologically dead. Hunter-gatherer bands were more likely to abandon their sick than to succor them (p. 31).

Figure 2.1　Sir William Osler. One of the great men of American medicine at the turn of the 20th century, Osler was a prime figure in medical education, a scholar of medical history, and a philosopher. He was a founder of the Johns Hopkins Medical School.

In societies that adopt taboos with respect to ritual purity—for example, the ancient Hebrews and Indian Brahmanism—disease and death were considered defiling impurities. Their approach to disease was generally to ostracize the individual until well again (Preuss, 1978).

Aversive behavior limits access to medical care. It may be argued that both Christianity and Buddhism developed in part as polemical responses to the early Judaic and Brahmanic cultures from which they split off, respectively, in an effort to provide compassionate care for the sick. But the risks of contagion and premature death limit the adaptive advantages of caring for the sick. For this reason, one cannot reliably expect sickness behavior to trigger medical attention.

Eliciting Concern

The communication of sickness behavior neither assures that someone will be available to offer treatment nor, alternatively, that he or she will be qualified to do so. Professional healers must be trained and willing to approach patients who are ill under adverse, and at times life-threatening, circumstances. This is their social contract with the sick.

In summer 1976, I was a medical intern in Philadelphia, when a number of people attending the American Legion Convention presented to the hospital with a rapidly progressive and often fatal pneumonia later termed Legionnaire's disease. At the time, no one knew what caused the disease—only that it appeared to be communicable.

The medical staff suppressed its fears of contracting this mysterious illness while attending to extremely sick patients. Although the disease did not spread to health-care workers—the pathogenic bacteria had infected the Legionnaires via a contaminated common water source—in other epidemics, physician deaths are not uncommon. Yet, failure to minister to the sick due to concerns for one's own welfare is as unacceptable for a physician as cowardice is for a soldier on the battlefield.

Whether sickness is effectively communicated can determine whether treatment is subsequently offered. Patients who suffer from disorders that show discordance between subjective symptoms and the observable signs of disease can encounter difficulties eliciting compassionate care. This is a frequent plaint of patients with psychosomatic disorders, who report feeling ill but generally do not appear sick. Family members, friends, and even doctors often tend to ignore or make light of their symptoms. In fact, the history of the placebo response is inextricably linked to this group of patients.

Healing

As Cousins (1995) noted, the placebo response is an innate mode of healing. *To heal* is to make sound and whole. Healing functions by restoring something that has been lost— either a part of the body or an important physiological process. Healing is also automatic, as anyone who has healed from a disease knows. It requires neither volition nor effort. Whether particular mindsets can promote or detract from healing remains controversial, but the following anecdote is worthy of consideration.

Some years ago, I directed a clinical trial of an innovative form of cancer immunotherapy. The trial received widespread attention, and many patients with advanced cancer were eager to enroll in it. Some were well informed with respect both to their disease and to the available options for treatment. This group was generally inquisitive and eager to participate in the treatment. At the time, I was referred a patient with a highly aggressive form of kidney cancer that had spread to his lungs. He was likable but taciturn, displaying little apparent interest either in his disease or in the details of his treatment. Efforts by the staff to engage him in his care evoked little enthusiasm. However, his usual response was simply, "Doc, you're the expert, so go ahead and do whatever you think is best." He exhibited substantial faith in doctors and in the healthcare team.

The treatment included the intravenous injection of inter-leukin-2 (IL-2), a cytokine that evokes a flu-like illness as a side effect. I had come to view this as evidence that the treatment was working, although it by no means assured that tumors would respond. But this patient was unique; he did not develop a fever or report feeling unwell. For 10 days, he appeared physiologi-cally inured to the daily treatments, and I recall thinking at the time that he would certainly prove to be a treatment failure. So I was astonished when subsequent chest radiographs showed that the massive tumors in his lungs had completely disappeared. He received the good news with characteristically muted enthusi-asm; he thanked me, and did well for some time before his can-cer unfortunately eventually recurred.

By contrast, virtually all of the patients who had been enthu-siastically engaged in their treatment—practicing guided imag-eries, supplementing their diets with vitamins and nutraceuticals, and tracking of all of the details of their treatment—showed no reduction in their burden of tumor. Was this a coincidence?

Psychologist Mihaly Csikszentmihalyi (1990) argued in *Flow: The Psychology of Optimal Experience* that certain physiological responses are optimized by the absence of conscious attention. Athletes, actors, musicians, and others routinely report that self-consciousness detracts from the level of their performance. Might healing also be one of these activities? Is the mind–body integration that healing represents potentially inhibited by excessive conscious attention? Indeed, does the absence of self-reflection in other animals contribute to their apparently extraordinary capacities to heal? The answers are not known, but the questions are worth pondering. Obviously, there might have been innumerable other reasons that the patients in this study did not develop positive antitumor responses. Even if conscious attention were a factor, it is currently impossible to comment intelligently on how it played a role. But the question deserves unbiased critical examination.

Modern man tends to place great stock in the powers of consciousness, and to suggest that it might be a problem can seem almost heretical to some. The idea that participating actively in one's therapy might, like so many things, have both positive and negative effects is not currently a popular stance. But why society has witnessed increased emphasis on agency and self-sufficiency is a topic that bears further consideration. I suspect that few patients today can, like the patient I described, express unwavering faith in their physicians. Might the increasing emphasis on self-help in today's society actually detract from therapeutic benefits by inhibiting the placebo response?

In a paper titled "Great Expectations: Evolutionary Psychology of Faith Healing and the Placebo Effect," British psychologist Nicholas Humphrey (2002) argued that the placebo response is triggered by a surge of hope and faith, elements that have suffered a serious setback in secular societies. Is it possible that rationality is at odds not only with feelings, as psychotherapists have long recognized, but also with the healing capacities of the body?

Placebo Or Not? That Is the Question

The clinical trial that I have just described presents an excellent opportunity for pondering how difficult it can be to determine what is a therapeutic effect in the absence of rigorous controls. The mode of cancer immunotherapy that was being evaluated eventually proved to be modestly active, and elements of it continue to be used in the treatment of certain chemotherapy-resistant cancers. However, the study did not include a placebo group. It was a "phase II trial", in which a relatively small group of patients were treated and response rates and side effects noted. But in the absence of a control group, the question persists as to whether the cancer responses were placebo effects.

At the time, when a senior oncologist raised that possibility, I respectfully dismissed it. To my mind, placebo effects might confound a chemotherapy trial, but this treatment included cancer surgery, and the isolation of tumor-infiltrating lympho-cytes that were grown in the laboratory and then injected back into the patient together with IL-2 (Kradin et al., 1989). The trial had been carefully designed, was based on a sound mechanism, had been laboriously proved to work in laboratory animals, and was so complex that it was inconceivable to me that it might be a placebo effect. Furthermore, the treatment yielded substan-tial side effects. These features did not fit my limited "sugar-pill" concept of a placebo as inert and nonspecific. However, having investigated the scope of placebo effects, I confess to no longer being sure. Despite the fact that reported placebo cures of cancer are rare, neither the nature of the disease, the complexity of the treatment, nor its rational basis can exclude the possiblility of placebo effects.

Indeed, the spectrum of responses seen in response to the administration of a placebo is wide. In a review of 15 studies that included 1,082 patients who received placebos, Dr. Henry Beecher (1955) observed responses in wound pain, seasickness, headaches, coughs, and anxieties. Other disorders known to respond to placebos have included arthritis, ulcers, hypertension, warts, and, yes, cancer.

Healing Versus Cure

Although the terms *healing* and *cure* are often used interchange-ably, they should be properly distinguished. A patient with lung cancer may be cured by surgery by completely excising his tumor, but the loss of his lung can leave him chronically short of breath and not healed. Doctors cure; nature heals. As such, placebo responses also do not cure; they heal. But even this distinction grants too much credit to therapeutic interventions, as there is no cure that does not rely on healing. Yet the contribution of healing is often given short shrift, particularly in the aggressive practice of medicine. The following clinical anecdote underscores the point.

A patient with acute leukemia was treated with chemotherapy in the hope of eradicating the malignant white cells in her bone marrow. Unfortunately, the side effects of her therapy included the temporary loss of her immune response. As a result, she subsequently developed a life-threatening opportunistic fungal infection in her lungs. She was appropriately treated with a number of strong antibiotics but continued to do poorly. When members of the medical team declared that they were perplexed by her poor response, a senior clinician exclaimed, "What do you expect? All of the antibiotics in the world won't cure her if her immune system isn't working!"

Consider how extraordinary healing actually is. Cut yourself, and by the next morning a scab will have formed. If the cut is not too deep, in several weeks there will be no evidence that the injury ever occurred. Did you consciously will this? Did attention promote the wound healing in any way? Obviously, the answer is no. Often all that is required for healing is a good night's sleep. But now suppose that the gash was deep enough to require stitches. In this situation, a surgeon must clean the wound, approximate its edges, and close it with sutures. These are important interventions, because without them bleeding, infection, and scarring can ensue. Yet once the wound has been closed, the cure depends entirely on healing. Drugs, surgeries, and other man-made technologies have unquestionably greatly improved the prognosis for many diseases; but these interventions merely prime the pump for the body to heal itself, and unless these innate healing processes are intact, a cure will not ensue.

We rely on nature because the processes of healing are so numerous and so complex that we have only begun to scratch the surface of how they actually work. When I first began my study of immunology almost 30 years ago, there was one known cytokine. Currently, there are scores of them, and new ones continue to be discovered. Furthermore, cytokines are only one small piece of the great jigsaw puzzle of healing. There are clotting proteins, complement molecules, white cells, antibodies, and chemokines, all working in concert. As evolutionary biologists Randolph Nesse and George Williams (1996) suggest, "These repair processes show a precise, complex coordination that a symphony orchestra might well envy. Unfortunately, no one has yet written the score for the healing symphony" (p. 70).

I often chuckle when I attend scientific meetings because there are invariably scientists in attendance who are enthusiastically promoting the importance of a newly discovered protein

Table 2.1   Mechanisms of Spontaneous Healing in Man

Intracellular repair of genetic mutations

Cellular immune responses

Humoral immune responses

Blood clotting

Wound healing

Expulsion of infectious agents by cough, vomiting, defecation

that they claim may someday explain how disease develops and should be treated. A colleague refers to this as the *molecule du jour*. Fads are not limited to Hollywood, as each year, some area of science comes into focus. But, by the following year, the field has invariably moved on, leaving the now old discovery to be tediously examined for its actual role in disease.

Contemplating the magnitude of the body's processes evokes genuine feelings of awe and humility, comparable to appreciating the number of stars in the sky on a clear night. Lest the reader become concerned that I may be arguing for intelligent design, I must confess to being agnostic with respect to nature's authorship. But consider the following: It has taken all of evolution, via trial and error, countless millions of years, beginning with the earliest primordial spontaneous creation of an amino acid up to the appearance of *Homo sapiens,* to develop systems of healing, like the placebo response, that are adapted to the well-being of man.

Next, consider the fact that medical science has been in a position to develop rational therapeutic interventions for approximately 200 years. The ability to distinguish a mechanistically specific drug from a placebo has been available for less than 100 years. It is obvious that man has much catching up to do. The family physician of my youth once made the following comment while visiting on what is now a rarity—a house call. On receiving his fee, he quipped, "God heals; doctors collect the fee!" It is still a sage observation.

3 A Brief History of Medicine and the Changing Implications of Placebos

> Medicine is the most distinguished of all the arts, but through the ignorance of those who practice it and of those who casually judge such practitioners, it is now of all the arts by far the least esteemed.
>
> **Hippocrates**

Introduction

Until relatively recent times, virtually all therapeutic interventions were placebos. How then did the specfic concept of a placebo develop? The answer has much to do with how we imagine the physical world, including health and disease. It is difficult for a scientifically minded individual to envision how medicine might have evolved along different paths than the one that currently dominates practice. But there have always been competing theories of disease causation and differences of opinion as to what constitutes effective therapy.

The Scientific Approach

We owe our current scientific emphasis on observation of the material world to the ancient Greek philosophers. Thales, the first recognized Greek philosopher, opined that the universe was made of water. Centuries later, Aristotle was concerned with categorizing the natural world around him. His father was a physician, and Aristotle expressed a keen interest in biology and in the human body. As a natural scientist, his approach to the material world was based on what could be gleaned via the senses, in contrast to the Platonic emphasis on immaterial ideal forms. Alexander of Macedon who conquered the known world in the fourth century was tutored by Aristotle and introduced his philosophy to the Hellenized world (Robinson, 1995).

Mentally, one can draw an arrow, with its origin located in Aristotle, extending through the Roman physician Galen, the anatomist Vesalius, the Enlightenment physiologist Harvey, and terminating in the medical science of our day. Along this path, one will identify a consistent philosophical perspective rooted in empirical observation as well as in the idea of reducing the object of scientific analysis—the case in point here being the human body—progressively into its smaller constituents for the purposes of determining its function.

The analytic approach to the body is based on the method of dissection—that is, on separating its parts, one from the other, with the express purpose of examining them in isolation. Indeed, all physicians in the West are taught that structure is the basis of function and that the two are inextricably bound together. The belief motivating this approach—and I am purposeful in applying the term *belief* rather than *idea*—is that if the body can be examined at progressively smaller scales, then scientists will be able to explain its activities and to devise new cures for disease. This mode of reductionism has been the basis of the great critical success of medical therapeutics up to the present time. But it has serious shortcomings that have impeded progress in some critical areas.

For one, the idea that there is always a deeper cause capable of explaining the behavior of matter may not be correct. Making this point is relatively easy, as all one need do is to consider any material object by progressively reducing it in size, as physicists have tended to do. What one is left with is a host of subatomic particles. Certainly, a bucket of quarks can tell very little about the behavior of, for example, a red blood cell. Emphasizing ever smaller scales of structure and function invariably leads to the problem of missing the forest for the trees. This is especially true if one's interest requires intact human being, like the placebo response. Whereas details at ever smaller scales of observation are interesting and potentially important, a different scientific approach is required to integrate such details back to the level of the behavior of the object as a whole. Activities, like the placebo response, cannot be explained by interminable reductionism but instead require a synthetic approach capable of predicting integrated behavior.

Criticisms of medical reductionism must not be misconstrued as arguments favoring the current holistic medical models. Emphasizing the human as a whole is not necessarily holistic or even primarily a humanistic goal; rather, it reflects the recognition that the intact human being is a legitimate object worthy of sophisticated scientific study. As science, most holistic approaches have serious limitations. They lack explanatory power and generally include no convincing mechanistic underpinnings. It is virtually impossible to make accurate predictions based on their views. Furthermore, they fail to meet an accepted criterion of a science, which is the ability to connect with other bodies of scientific information in a productive way. In Western science, the definitive goal has been to construct links to physics, because of the latter's extraordinary explanatory power and its unusual level of success in adopting mathematics as its language. No holistic model for medicine currently meets these criteria.

Although the goals of holistic practices are appealing, most scientists in the West have rejected them for the reasons stated. But as new modalities of scientific inquiry emerge that are able to describe the behavior of integrated complex systems while still meeting the criteria of scientific credibility, it may soon be possible to include the aims of holistic approaches within the scientific container. To appreciate how the placebo response has evolved, it will be necessary to explore how its history tracks in parallel with that of medical science. What will become evident is that perspectives on the placebo response have been determined by evolving ideas as to what constitutes medical science.

Placebo, Shamanism, and Healing

The practice of medicine likely developed in prehistoric cultures along the lines of what modern anthropologists have called *shamanism*. The shaman, according to anthropologist Mircea Eliade (1964), acquires his position in traditional societies in one of several ways. One may inherit it by virtue of having being born into a family of shamans. Others learn their trade as apprentices. But for some, the profession is a vocation—that is, a true calling. According to Eliade, this type of shaman generally begins his career after being stricken by what might be termed a *schizophreniform illness*. While in a trance-like altered state of consciousness, the proto-shaman may describe leaving his body to travel to distant worlds or, alternatively, being hacked to pieces and magically spontaneously reassembled. Such experiences would undoubtedly be labeled as psychotic in our society, but in the world of the shaman these harrowing subjective events are purposeful, as they give rise to a mature healer shaman who is prepared to minister to others.

The shaman embodies the archetypal idea of the wounded healer that is encountered in virtually all cultures. The initiatory illness imbues the shaman not only with power (*mana*) but also with the firsthand experience of what it means to be sick to the point of death. This evokes compassion and empathy, two of the cardinal features that promote placebo healing. In the shamanic model, disease is viewed either as a loss of soul or as an uninvited possession by demonic forces. Modern medicine continues to include these core imaginings as part of its beliefs but has reworked them. As in shamanic practice, therapy is based on supplying an antidote by repletion of what has been lost (e.g., blood transfusion) or, alternatively, by extracting what one has been possessed by via, for example, emetics, or surgeries. Shamanic healing is distinguished by the gross asymmetry of the therapeutic relationship in which the shaman provides the power and expertise to effect healing and in which the patient responds out of a profound belief in these powers. This asymmetric dynamic has been repeated throughout the history of medicine, and it may be an essential feature of placebo healings.

The Paleolithic fossil record suggests that prehistoric shamanic practices may have included the earliest surgical interventions (Majno, 1975). Trephining, a method of boring a hole into the skull (Figure 3.1), has been suggested as physical evidence of a neurosurgical procedure aimed at relieving intracranial pressure in hunters who had developed intracranial bleeding following blunt head injury. Unfortunately, the fossil record is also a blank screen for the projections of researchers, as this procedure might just as well have been a method of releasing "evil spirits" from the possessed patient's skull.

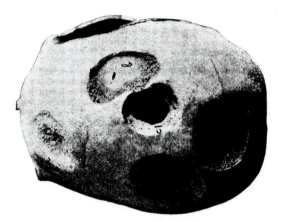

Figure 3.1   Trephined skull. A Paleolithic skull shows numerous bore-holes. The rationale for this procedure is uncertain. It may have been either a primitive neurosurgical technique or a mode of releasing an evil spirit from a possessed patient.

The Role of Magic and Religion in Placebo Healing

It is difficult for modern man to appreciate a theory of disease that is based wholly in superstition. But magic played the dominant role in medicine from prehistory well through the Middle Ages. As in shamanic practice, to which it is related, the charismatic personality and perceived power of the healer was the active ingredient in magico-religious placebo healing. Magical healing included the use of amulets and incantations, phrases that carried powers known only to those initiated in their application. As medical historian Julius Preuss (1978) noted in his text, *Biblical and Talmudic Medicine,* physicians in ancient times often used incantations, with each malady calling for a specific incantation that would counter its effects. Even the Roman physician Galen, who was grounded in the rationalist tradition of Aristotle, opined in favor of their application:

> Some people believe that incantations are equivalent to fairy tales of old women. I too thought this way for a long time. As time passed, however, I became convinced of the value of incantations because of their apparent efficacy (Temkin, p 234).

Magical practices developed in early Egyptian and Mesopotamian civilizations. Magical medical papyri have survived in Egypt, and apotropaics have been widely discovered in the Near East, mostly in the form of execration tablets (Majno, 1975). In addition, both the New and Old Testament are replete with examples of magical healings. Difficulties arise in attempting to distinguish magical from religious practices, and as Matthew Dickie (2003), a scholar of ancient magical practices, has suggested, the distinction is largely in the eye of the beholder. Traditionally most religions have frowned officially on magical practices despite their widespread popularity. Jewish Levitical law and Christian canon law both call for harsh penalties for those who practice as diviners, soothsayers, or necromancers, as well as for those who seek out their skills, as King Saul did with the Witch of Endor in Samuel I (Coogan, 2001). Even the nonmonotheistic and nondoxological tradition of Theravadin Buddhism frowns on the practice of magic (Bodhi, 2000).

Until the post-Reformation witch trials, Christianity was reserved in its punishments of those who practiced or sought out magic for the purpose of healing. The practice of magical healing was so widespread in the Roman Empire of the fourth century as to motivate Eastern church father John Chrysostom to admonish Christians for continuing to attend the synagogues in hope of being cured by Jewish magical practices (Dickie, 2003).

There may be other reasons for the silence of the church with respect to magical healing, as eminent historian of Christianity Morton Smith (1978) has suggested. In his text *Jesus the Magician,* Smith argued that the historical Jesus was best characterized as an itinerant charismatic practitioner of magic. Jesus' career, according to Smith, included precisely the types of activities practiced by the magicians of his time: healing the sick, raising the dead, multiplying food, walking on water, and transforming water into wine. Such extraordinary feats, although uncommon, were not unique in ancient times. At least two Old Testament prophets, Elijah and Elisha, had raised the dead, and many feats attributed to the late first-century Roman magician Apollonius of Tyana rivaled those of Jesus.

The Gospel texts support the notion that Jesus' following was inspired primarily by his practices of healing the sick and raising the dead, rather than by his teachings. Indeed, according to Mathew 11: 4–5, when questioned as to whether he was the Messiah by the followers of John the Baptist, Jesus admonished them to return to John with the message that "the sick are healed and the dead are raised," affirming the power of his ministry. If one accepts these feats and ignores their theological implications, they can be interpreted as extraordinary placebo effects.

Evidence can be found in the Gospel narratives (Luke 8:48) of the critical importance of the asymmetry of the therapeutic dynamic. Faith in the power of the healer is paramount. On several occasions, Jesus actually remarks, "Your faith has healed you." Furthermore, as Smith (1978) noted, there are several references within the Gospels to occasions when Jesus failed in his efforts to heal the sick, and these are attributed to a lack of faith. In Mark 6:2, Jesus was unable to perform miracles in his hometown of Nazareth:

> What kinds of miracles do his hands do? Isn't this the carpenter, the son of Mary, and the brother of James and Joseph and Judah and Simon? And aren't his sisters here with us? ... And he could not do any miracle there. And he [Jesus] marveled at their unbelief.

Jesus, in turn, complained in Matthew 13:57, "A prophet is not without honor, but in his own country, and among his own kin, and in his own house." From the perspective of modern biblical textual criticism, these passages are likely to represent a veridical strand in the Gospels, as they oppose the polemical claim of the Gospel authors that Jesus was able to create miracles independent of the attitudes of others. It is remarkable to consider the possibility that the placebo response may be the basis of the dominant religions of the Western world.

Medicine and the Greeks

The roots of the Western medical scientific tradition are widely attributed to the ancient Greeks (Porter, 2002). It is possible to trace Greek medical thought from an early magico-religious period to an embryonic empirical science. But healing in both was ultimately attributed to the gods. According to ancient Greek myth, Asklepios (Figure 3.2) was the son of a mortal woman, Coronis, and the god Apollo. Asklepios learns his skills as a healer from Chiron, who is referred to as a wounded healer. The centaur-as-healer motif symbolizes the Greeks' recognition that animal instinct is a chthonic factor in healing.

Asklepios exhibits exceptional healing powers as the first physician, culminating in his ability to raise the dead. But when Hades — who rules the dead in the Underworld — protests that his realm is becoming depopulated, Asklepios is killed by Zeus's thunderbolt, and subsequently elevated to the level of a god at the behest of Apollo (Graves, 1988).

A cultic system of healing practices developed around the myth of Asklepios and enjoyed wide popularity. Asklepian temples dotted the Greek Isles and the coast of Asia Minor. These temples were sites of religious ritual and healing. In many respects, they resembled modern spas, (Figure 3.3), where sick patients were encouraged to partake in activities designed to soothe mind and body. These included visiting the baths and sacrificing to Asklepios. Patients were isolated overnight in

Figure 3.2 Asklepios. The first physician, according to Greek myth, he is depicted here with a caduceus, an early symbol of medical practice that has persisted until modern times.

incubation chambers for the purpose of encouraging dreams (Edelstein & Edelstein, 1945). The early inscriptions that describe the rituals indicate that Asklepios appeared in the dream and healed the patient directly. However, in later accounts, his role was reduced to offering the prescription for what was required to effect healing. The following day, a physician visited the sick

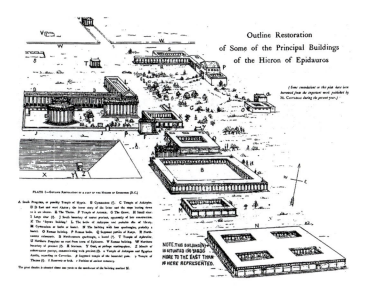

Figure 3.3 Asklepian Temple. Asklepian temples dotted the Mediterranean and resembled a modern-day spa. The figure shows the layout of the temple at Epidaurus, located in contemporary Greece. Asklepian rituals include many of the factors thought to evoke placebo effects, including relaxing baths, sacrifice to Asklepios, and an incubation chamber designed to promote dreams.

patient and proceeded to assist in filling the prescription (Meir, 1968). At the end of the stay, as in a modern spa, the patient was required to pay a hefty fee.

These descriptions are among the earliest detailed accounts of healing in the ancient world. Based on extant testimonials, many patients responded well to the treatment. For this reason, the elements of these rituals might shed light on how placebo effects were evoked at that time. As noted, the Asklepian rites included (1) isolating the patient; (2) engaging him in activities designed to promote relaxation; (3) a display of religious devotion via the sacrifice; (4) attention to dreams; (5) meeting with a physician; and (6) payment of a fee.

Isolation recapitulates sickness behavior and reduces exposure to extraneous stimuli that contribute to stress. The soothing baths augment relaxation. Sacrificing to Asklepios was a symbolic act of devotion to the power of the god. In ancient times, dreams were considered messages from the gods, whereas today, they are ascribed to the brain activities during rapid eye movement sleep (Kradin, 2006). The Asklepian prescription for healing demanded an attitude toward the dream that included receptivity to mental imagery and unconscious processes. The physician's role in the ritual was not primarily to intervene with standard treatments for what ailed the patient, as it is now, but rather to foster the specific healing process prescribed in the dream by participating in an interpersonal dynamic that could evoke the placebo response. Finally, the payment of the fee confirmed that something of value had transpired and helped to consolidate therapeutic gains.

The Asklepian ritual was a precursor of scientific medical therapeutics. It was a transitional mode of therapeutics, located between ancient magico-religious rites and an emerging practice based on empirical observation. Both of these perspectives persist in modern medicine as the *art* and *science* of therapeutics, respectively. However, this characterization tends to impede recognition that the art of medicine is also science, albeit one that includes elements not usually examined by medical scientists. However, modern psychologists would have little difficulty in recognizing these "artful" elements as legitimate objects of objective investigation.

Hippocrates and Medical Empiricism

The first scientific healing practices have been attributed to Hippocrates and his school. However, comparable systems of diagnosis and treatment were developing concomitantly on the Indian subcontinent and in China. The core principles of Buddhist practice and religion, the Four Noble Truths, were formulated as a medical stratagem of diagnosis and treatment and the Buddha is often depicted in iconography (Figure 3.4), like Jesus, as a healer (Avedon et al., 1998).*

Hippocrates of Cos (c.450 BCE; Figure 3.5) was a contemporary of Socrates and, according to hagiography, a descendent of Asklepios. However, the Hippocratic approach to healing, unlike that of the Asklepians, was rooted in empirical observation. The Hippocratic treatises are distinguished by carefully formulated sets of descriptions of disease, many of which remain

---

* The Four Noble Truths are paraphrased here as follows: (1) There is suffering; (2) there is a cause of suffering; (3) there is a treatment for suffering; and (4) the outline of the treatment is the Noble Eightfold Path. This is essentially the practice of recognizing the disease: diagnosing its cause, estimating the prognosis, and providing a prescription. The Buddha is often referred to in the Buddhist scriptures as a physician.

Figure 3.4   Medicine Buddha: The Buddha is often depicted iconograph-
ically as a healer. Invariably he is blue, in a seated position, and holding a
medicine bowl. The Four Nobel Truths of Buddhism are formulated as a
diagnosis, prognosis, and prescription.

relevant to modern practice. Interestingly, the primary focus of
the Hippocratic School was not on therapeutics but on establishing prognosis—that is, the ability to accurately predict the
outcome of a disease.

But if therapeutic benefits were mainly attributable to
placebo effects, how were they fostered by this approach? The

Figure 3.5   Hippocrates of Cos. The figure shows an ancient Greek bust of Hippocrates. A contemporary of Socrates, Hippocrates' practice of medicine was based on careful observation of the natural history of disease. The emphasis of the Hippocratic School on knowledge rather than magic was the source of medical science as we know it today.

Hippocratic School placed diminished emphasis on the methods of the magico-religious tradition. However, placebo healings were based on the asymmetric therapeutic dynamic between Hippocratic physician and patient. This was no longer based on the charisma and magical power of the healer; instead, it centered on the physician's knowledge and professional virtues. The requirement for virtue is revealed in the Hippocratic Oath that is still recited by physicians upon graduation from medical school:

> … I will give no deadly medicine to anyone if asked, nor suggest any such counsel; and in like manner I will not give to a woman a pessary to produce abortion. With purity and with holiness I will pass my life and practice my art.…

The Hippocratic physician derived his power from knowledge and practiced observation, comparable to physicians today. A quotation attributed directly to Hippocrates captures this new spirit with respect to the art of medical practice:

> I say we ought not to reject the ancient Art, as if it were not, and had not been properly founded, because it did not attain accuracy in all things, but rather since it is capable of reaching to the greatest exactitude by reasoning, to receive it and admire its discoveries, made from a great state of ignorance, and as having been well and properly made, and not from chance.… (Osler, p. 218)

The faith previously displayed by patients in their magical healers was transfigured into a robust belief in the power of the rational healer.

The Hippocratic treatises include numerous descriptions of diseases as well as medical and surgical procedures. Unlike the

Asklepian ritual, they represent a stream of Greek thought rooted in a materialistic philosophy with emphasis on the Pythagorean concept of balance and harmony (Robinson, 1995). According to the Hippocratic School, the normal function of the body depended on the balance of four humors: blood, choler, phlegm, and black bile (Porter, 1997). These corresponded to the four cardinal Aristotelian elements of air, fire, water, and earth and to the parallel cardinal quaternity of hot, cold, wet, and dry. Aristotle's treatises on the materiality of the body were to guide the direction of medical therapeutics through the Middle Ages. Indeed, this approach was a source of controversy even in Hippocrates' time. Plato complained, "... The great error of our day in the treatment of the human body [is that] physicians separate the soul and the body" (Plato, p. 11).

Disease was not attributed primarily to structural abnormalities but to an imbalance of humors. Healing was sought via the restoration of humoral balance. An example from the *Aphorisms of Hippocrates* reveals how this idea shaped therapeutic rationale (Hippocrates, 1964):

> During the increase of the body, there is the greatest increase of internal heat: more food is required to prevent its consumption. But in the old there is less heat; [so that] less food is therefore required (p. 17).

However, Aristotle's system was also metaphysical. Nature was observed directly, but discerning its purpose (*telos*) was of great importance. An imbalance of humors was often a matter of a disturbance in the patient's underlying temperament, and it is from this idea that our descriptions of individuals as choleric, phlegmatic, sanguine, or melancholic are derived. Balance was the cardinal goal of most Greco-Roman philosophies, as it contributed both to a virtuous life and good health. Redressing the one-sidedness of the personality was the therapeutic goal.

The Ancient Medical Armamentarium: The Placebo Pharmacopeia

The ancients recognized the narcotic effects of poppy and the soporific effects of wine and cannabis, but the litany of drugs and other treatments listed in the oldest known records of pharmacopoeia, the Egyptian Ebers Papyrus and the Babylonian cuneiform inscriptions, would all currently be judged placebos (Shapiro & Shapiro, 1997). Certain herbal medications with specific pharmacological activities (e.g., Ma Huang or ephedra) were administered in ancient China but possibly not in schedules that would have been therapeutic. In fact, as far as can be ascertained, the ancient therapeutic armamentarium included very few active treatments. Most were based on rituals of bleeding, diuresis, and purging, none of which would pass muster as effective today.

If virtually all ancient medical treatments were placebos, how did mankind manage to survive the prescientific era? But survive it did, providing evidence for the efficacy of the placebo response. It is uncertain when the idea of treating patients with medicines first developed, but Sir William Osler (1921), a towering figure in medical education, referred to man as the only animal who self-medicates, i.e, man is innately both *Homo sapiens* and *Homo medicamentosum.*

By the 17th century, the European Reformation had largely broken the hold of the Catholic Church and of medieval scholasticism. As a result, the influences of religion, magic, and the Aristotelian worldview were seriously questioned for the first time in more than a millennium. The scientific revolution began in earnest in the 15th century with Copernicus's challenge to the Ptolemaic geocentric worldview. However, it reached its zenith with the discoveries of Isaac Newton (Figure 3.6).

It is impossible to overestimate the effect that Newton's discoveries had on how man viewed his world. For the first time, major parts of the physical universe, including the motion of the heavenly bodies, could be accurately described and predicted without recourse to metaphysical claims. But medicine lagged behind. French philosopher Rene Descartes said the following:

> It is true that the medicine which is now in vogue contains little of which the utility is remarkable, but without having any intention of decrying it, I am sure that there is no one, even amongst those who make its study a profession, who does not confess that all that men know is almost nothing in comparison to what remains to be known.... (Osler, p. 15).

However, a progressively enlightened population did decry the nonscientific methods of medical practice. They grew to be increasingly objects of derision, with physicians often seen as meddlesome and dangerous. The deathbed scene of King Charles

Figure 3.6   Sir Isaac Newton. Undoubtedly the most influential scientific figure in history, Newton's insights into nature and mathematics have dominated science since the 17th century. All of the natural sciences are bound to his formulations of classical mechanics, with roots in causality and reductionism.

II of Great Britain in the late 17th century underscores reasons for such opinions (Porter, 1998, p 234):

> Sixteen ounces of blood were removed in his right arm with immediate good effect. As was the approved practice of the time, the King was

allowed to remain in the chair in which the convulsions seized him; his teeth were held forcibly open to prevent him biting his tongue; the regimen was … "first to get him to wake, and then to keep him from sleeping." Urgent messages had been dispatched to the King's numerous personal physicians, who quickly came flocking to his assistance; they were summoned regardless of distinctions of creed and politics, and they came. They ordered cupping glasses to be applied to his shoulders forthwith, and deep scarification to be carried out by which they succeeded in removing another eight ounces of blood. A strong antimonial emetic was administered, but as the King could be got to swallow only a small portion of it, they determined to render assurance doubly sure by a full dose of Sulphate of Zinc. Strong purgatives were given, and supplemented by a succession of clysters. The hair was shorn close and pungent blistering agents were applied all over his head; and as though this was not enough the red-hot cautery was requisitioned as well.

Suffice it to say, the king died shortly thereafter.

The Advent of Pharmaceutical Science and the Changing Role of Placebo

Arguably, it was not until the 18th century that the first unequivocally nonplacebo drug was identified (Shapiro & Shapiro, 1997). Quinine, an extract from Cinchona bark, proved to be an effective antimalarial agent, as only malarial fevers but not other febrile illnesses responded to its properties. Aspirin, derived from the bark of the white willow tree, was noted have antipyretic and anti-inflammatory effects in 1763 (Evans, 2004). But despite the importance of these discoveries, they were sporadic observations.

The formal scientific investigation of pharmacology did not become routine until the 19th century, when French physician Magendie performed experiments demonstrating that the emetic properties of ipecacuanha (ipecac) were attributable to a specific chemical substance he termed emetine (Shapiro & Shapiro, 1997). A rash of subsequent experimentation demonstrated the activities of a variety of alkaloids, including strychnine, nicotine, and atropine. These drugs were developed through a new approaches that combined medicinal chemistry with physiological experimentation. Scientists developed the notion that drugs should have both specific and predictable activities. Consider this statement by Pierre Louis (1834) in his *Essay on Clinical Instruction*:

> As to different methods of treatment it is possible for us to assure ourselves of the superiority of one or another ... by enquiring if the greater number of individuals have been cured by one means or another. Here it is necessary to count (Evans, p 6).

Whereas medical treatments of earlier times (e.g., the application of leeches, toxic purging) offend current sensibilities, it is important to appreciate that modern man has been the benefactor of a long tradition of scientific reasoning, which was not the case in times past. Furthermore, as we have seen, it is a mistake to infer that rationality predicts therapeutic efficacy. Treatments that are held in disdain today surely held meaning for both physicians and patients in times past. But with the emergence of the new scientific attitude, the irrational methods of the past were challenged. The faith required for eliciting placebo effects could no longer be reliably evoked by the old practices.

Placebo and the Age of Science

Placebo is the Latin Vulgate translation of the biblical Hebrew word *ethalekh,* meaning "I will go before" (Shapiro & Shapiro, 1997). With a somewhat different connotation, the term is found in the Vesper prayer that begins, *Placebo domino in regione vivorum* (I will please the Lord in the land of the living). This prayer was recited in medieval times by Catholic priests and at the time of the European Reformation in return for a fee, was seen increasingly as a practice that was symptomatic of the corruption in the Roman Church. The term was therefore imbued with pejorative implications that have continued.

As medical jargon, *placebo* first appears in Motherby's *New Medical Dictionary* in 1785, where it is defined as a "commonplace method or medicine" (Jackson, p. 280). By the end of the 18th century, the idea of a pedestrian nonscientific therapy required its own descriptor. Indeed, the idea of a placebo could only have arisen in a society that had divested itself of its proclivity for magical thinking. God's role in this brave new world was progressively limited to the salvation of human souls. The French scientist Pierre Laplace informed Napoleon that, in the wake of Newtonian thought, scientists no longer required divine assistance to explain the natural world.* Religion and science had come to an uncomfortable parting of the ways that continues to the present.

Medicine's divorce from religion was not always comfortable, and adopting a new mate in science would not be easy. If medicine were to establish equal footing with the older physical sciences, it would need to embrace a new approach, one based on evidence derived from experimentation. In the 19th century, Claude Bernard (1878), a distinguished medical scientist, argued that experimentation must serve as the basis for clinical therapeutics. Although the idea was widely received and led to substantial progress in the diagnosis and treatment of a host of disorders, from the vantage point of the physical sciences medicine was still overly metaphysical and lacking sufficient rigor. This stance was challenged in the 19th century by the pioneering research of Louis Pasteur in France and of the German scientist Robert Koch (Figure 3.7), who demonstrated via a series of elegant experiments that the bacterium *Mycobacteria tuberculosis* was the cause of the disease then ravaging Europe. Koch devised postulates that outlined how the cause of disease could be rigorously established. Koch's postulates continue to serve as the standard for scientific excellence in medicine, and Koch—a dispassionate observer who developed a hypothesis and then

---

* The preeminent scientist of his day, Sir Isaac Newton was far from a secularist. Instead, he was a profoundly religious man and an avid alchemist. His theological and alchemical works exceed the corpus of scientific writings that he is best remembered for.

Figure 3.7 Robert Koch. A great scientist, Koch introduced rigor into medical experimentation. He proved that tuberculosis was caused by a mycobacterium and developed the postulates that bear his name for establishing the cause of disease.

proceeded to test it by a well-controlled set of experiments—became the model of the medical scientist.

A Comparison of Medical and Physical Science: Similar But Not the Same

There are limits to the degree of experimental rigor that can be applied to human subjects. The design and conduct of experiments in the medical and physical sciences resemble each other, but only superficially. In the physical sciences, investigations are conducted under strict environmental conditions that include standardized temperatures and pressures. Experiments are repeated manifold to assure their accuracy. Only then—and after the findings have been reproduced by scientists in other laboratories—are results embraced by the scientific community.

Compare this with the conduct of a modern medical clinical trial in which a new drug or procedure is being evaluated. It is impossible to control rigorously for all of the differences in both the environment and the patients being examined. Whereas a well-designed trial will commonly include sufficient numbers of subjects to assure its statistical interpretation, this is not always the case. There is no possibility of repeating the trial with the same subjects and under the same condition. Whereas methods like randomization can reduce many of these the confounding elements, it is empirically true that the chances of reproducing the results of a clinical trial are low.

Why Is Medical Science Ambiguous?

Has the reader ever wondered why after so many years of investigation, medical scientists cannot agree on the answers to certain seemingly basic questions? A short list includes the following:

- Is estrogen replacement overall good or bad with respect to postmenopausal health?

- What is the role of diet and alcohol consumption in health?

- Which cancer operations yield the highest percentages of cure?

Rarely a week goes by without some new result reported in the medical literature that is subsequently widely popularized by the lay press, only to be refuted by another study at a later date. This cycle appears to have a life of its own, with few questioning why this might be the case.

Consider the recent controversy concerning the cardiac side effects of the popular arthritis drugs called COX-2 inhibitors. These drugs interfere with prostaglandins, molecules that cause inflammation, fever production, and blood clotting. Doctors have been unable to agree about the cardiac risks of these drugs, in part, because the results of clinical trials have differed substantially (Ozols, 2004).* One might conclude that evidence-based medicine, the current gold standard with respect to the conduct of medical practice—defined as "the explicit and judicious use of the current best evidence" (Kristiensen and Mooney 2004, p. 141) from clinical care research—may in reality be less than fully reliable.

---

* A reader who is interested in the details of this story is referred to the excellent monograph *Big Pharma* authored by journalist Jacky Law.

The Mind–Body Conundrum
and the Placebo Response

Historian of medicine Anne Harrington referred to the placebo response as an ambiguous phenomenon positioned between subjectivity and objectivity. In a recent text on the placebo response, physician W. Grant Thompson (2005) noted that it has been viewed historically alternatively as indefinable by philosophers, a source of culpability to bioethicists, and indispensable by some clinicians, as we have already examined. This level of ambiguity concerning the placebo response is indicative of a deeper underlying tension with respect to how the field of medicine approaches disease and its treatment. Jay Katz (1984) noted the following in *The Silent World of Doctor and Patient:*

> Modern medicine remains caught between science and intuition. This is not necessarily bad; indeed, medicine may have to be ruled by both science and intuition for a long time to come. What is disturbing though is that physicians are so reluctant to acknowledge to themselves and their patients which of their opinions and recommendations are based on science and which on intuition (p. 46).

The purposeful prescription of placebos developed in response to a perplexing challenge to medical therapeutics. Clinical medicine has, at least since modern times, included a substantial number of patients whose complaints have tended to defy rational explanation (Kradin, 1997). In his book *From Hysteria to Chronic Fatigue*, medical historian Edward Shorter (1993) concluded that patients with psychosomatic disorders have consistently accounted for roughly half of all medical consultations.

A distinguishing feature of psychosomatic disorders is their ability to change with the times—a feature shared by the placebo response. At the end of the 19th century, female patients might present to a physician complaining of anesthesia or the paralysis of a limb. Comparable symptoms were recognized as far back as Hippocrates and were attributed to hysteria, a disorder attributed to the aberrant migration of the uterus within the abdomen.* This meant that the disorder, although difficult to treat, was not beyond the limits of medical meaning to the ancients. But by the 19th century, physicians recognized that the anatomy of the nervous system could not possibly account for the reported symptoms; implying that either the symptoms or the patient was irrational.

Another common clinical syndrome in the 19th century was chronic fatigue termed neurasthenia and ascribed to a fundamental weakness of the nervous system.† Medicine still provides no good explanation for disabling fatigue in the absence of underlying disease, and this may explain why fatigue continues to be one of the most commonly observed psychosomatic symptoms in the modern clinic, currently labeled with the moniker *chronic fatigue syndrome.*

---

* The same root gives us the term *hysterectomy*, the surgical procedure in which the uterus is removed.

† This explanation may be closer to the truth, as there is evidence that chronic fatigue syndrome may result from instability of the hypothalamic-pituitary-adrenal axis.

The average medical practice at the end of the 19th century included large numbers of patients with intractable psychosomatic symptoms, none of which could be satisfactorily explained. As medical science grew more scientific psychosomatic symptoms were increasingly viewed by doctors either as symptoms of mental disease or as fictitious. This idea was fostered by French physician Pierre Charcot and Austrian neurologist (soon to become psychoanalyst) Sigmund Freud (Figure 3.8), in their claims that hysteria was primarily a derangement of mental activities rather than an organic disease of the nervous system.

Today, one rarely encounters the flamboyant cases of hysterical anesthesia and paralyses that once dominated medical practice (Kradin, 1997). Why this is the case is uncertain, but one distinct possibility is that patients might have become too medically sophisticated to develop them. Favoring this is the observation that comparable symptoms are still reported in societies where dissemination of medical information is limited. This is not to suggest that patients are purposely creating their symptoms; in fact, few would qualify as malingerers. Instead, it appears that the mind–brain unconsciously creates insoluble diagnostic and therapeutic dilemmas that can neither be dismissed nor resolved. The psychosomatic symptom is an extraordinary conundrum that continues to challenge medical science.

At the end of the 19th century, physicians in Europe and the United States were faced with an abundance of patients in their practices whom they could neither adequately diagnose nor

Figure 3.8 Sigmund Freud. The father of psychoanalysis, Freud was a neurologist with early interests in hysteria, which became the prototypic psychosomatic disorder. His idea of the negative therapeutic reaction shares many features with the negative placebo (nocebo) response.

treat. Physicians proposed a variety of diagnoses to explain the panoply of psychosomatic complaints, and the type of specialist consulted generally determined how they were formulated. As Shorter (1993) pointed out, patients with psychosomatic disorders tended either to seek out medical physicians, who passively supported their role as invalids, or surgeons, who actively addressed their woes by removing parts of their anatomy. Diagnoses of chronic appendicitis, colitis, and biliary duct spasm as causes of chronic constipation or vague abdominal pains emerged and were often treated by the removal of the offending organ, sometimes with excellent results. A hospital pathologist, whose task it was to describe the organs removed at surgery, searched for minor abnormalities to support the surgeon's preoperative diagnosis.*

Unfortunately, one's reputation as a healer and economic success can be undermined by therapeutic failures. Physicians searched for anything to prescribe that would offer their patients a modicum of relief. At the time, the available pharmacopoeia included a host of remedies that were of questionable benefit.† But the most controversial were those known by physicians, to be inert—that is, placebos.

It is understandable why physicians faced with an ailing and unhappy patient might choose to treat with a placebo. Economic self-preservation undoubtedly contributed to the widespread adoption of this practice, but it is unlikely that most physicians who prescribed placebos were intent on deceiving patients for

---

* I am old enough to have witnessed this at a premier academic medical center. Entire colons that were anatomically completely normal were occasionally removed for the treatment of constipation by an eminent surgeon. With the surgeon's death, this practice thankfully came to an end.

† Despite clinical trials designed to exclude ineffective drugs from the marketplace, this continues to be true today as well. Many current drugs are only barely, if at all, more effective than placebos.

their own gain. Instead, they knew, as did their prescientific forebears, that placebos yielded beneficial effects with regularity, even though no one had any idea as to how they might act. Furthermore, although medicine was increasingly viewed as a science, the average physician at the time was by no means a trained scientist. Indeed, it has only been since the early 1900s that doctors in the United States were required to have graduated from college; before this time, most learned their trade at the bedside (Shorter, 1985).

O. H. Pepper (1945) summed up the situation with respect to placebos as follows:

> The human mind is still open to suggestion, even in these modern and disillusioned days. The sympathetic physician will want to use every help for these pathetic patients and if the placebo can help, he will not neglect it. It cannot harm and may comfort and avoid the too quick extinction of opiate efficacy (p. 412).

However, ill will toward the use of placebos ran high in centers of academic medicine. Physicians were expected to serve two masters: one the traditional need of their patients, the other the increasing scientific standard of the profession. The towering figures of academic medical science demanded that these not be ignored in clinical practice. Richard Cabot (Figure 3.9) of Massachusetts General Hospital, who had once substituted a saline injection for morphine, only to be found out by his patient, became a crusading reformer for prohibiting the prescription of

Figure 3.9   Richard Cabot. A well-known figure in his day, Cabot practiced medicine at the Massachusetts General Hospital. He was a reformer and an ardent opponent of placebo administration.

placebos. Cabot equated this practice with quackery (Shorter, 1985).

But as Thompson (2005) pointed out, several types of placebo administration continue in practice (Table 3.1). As in Cabot's case, a clinician may choose purposefully to mislead a patient to elicit a salutary effect. Alternatively, a drug may be prescribed at a dosage that is ineffective or for a purpose for which its efficacy

Table 3.1   Types of Placebo Administration Observed in Clinical Practice

Purposeful prescription of inert drug (or other treatment)
Purposeful prescription of active drug at dosage that is ineffective
Purposeful prescription of active drug for purpose that it not efficacious
Unwitting prescription of drug that is ineffective

is unproven. But the most common mode of placebo may be the administration of a treatment that the doctor does not recognize as ineffective. It would require an enormous amount of time, money, and effort to prove that the current therapeutic armamentarium is effective at the spectrum of dosages and conditions for which it is currently employed. Medical practice swims in a sea of placebos and is none the wiser for it.

Limited knowledge of what is scientifically effective treatment leaves practitioners in an uncomfortable position. In Buddhist scripture there is a teaching simile in which a warrior is wounded by a poisoned arrow in battle (Bodhi, 2000). Physicians examine the wound and conclude that the patient can be saved if the arrow is removed immediately. But the warrior, a scientist at heart, insists on first knowing more details with respect to, for example, the wound, where the arrow is located, whether it is poisoned, as well as the kind of poison, before consenting to its removal. Of course, he dies before his questions can be answered. Therapy cannot always wait on science; at times action is required even when the scientific basis of that action is unknown. For this reason, physicians are reticent to abandon placebos, as Bailar (2001) insightfully noted, although they may wish to deny this, even to themselves.

Many lay people harbor the erroneous notion that physicians know how most treatments work. Truth be told, there is hardly an effective treatment in which the mechanism of action is well known, and in some cases, physicians have absolutely no idea as to how their prescriptions actually work. So to conclude that a mechanism is required for a treatment to be scientifically effective is untrue. Explanatory value is a critical feature of medical science, but it is not a necessary one. Treatments like homeopathy, patent medicine, and quackery, which were common less than a century ago, healed substantial numbers patients via placebo effects. Today, these have largely fallen into disrepute—but not as one might wish to believe because they are ineffective. In fact, questions of what constituted effective therapy at the turn of the last century were so confounded that it required legislation to establish orthodox therapeutic practices, because the public could not distinguish the therapeutic benefits of mainstream medicine from those of placebo treatments (Shorter, 1985).

The reader hopefully is beginning to grasp the complexity of discerning what constitutes effective therapy. If extricating placebo effects from the therapeutic effects of a so-called active intervention is impossible, how can one decide whether a new drug has activities that are not solely attributable to placebo effects? In the early 20th century, a thoughtful pharmacologist proposed a way out of this quagmire, and his suggestions initiated a new perspective on the placebos in medicine.

The Randomized Controlled Clinical Trial: Creating a New Role for Placebos

Prior to the 1940s, medical therapeutics was based on cumulative anecdotal observations of astute clinicians. However, the ubiquitous presence of placebo effects complicated the task of accounting for what was actually responsible for the observed therapeutic responses. A therapeutic effect, T_E, may be considered to be the sum of (1) the positive effects due to the specific actions of a drug, surgery, or psychological intervention, T_M and (2) the effects of the placebo response, T_P, so that

$$T_E = T_M + T_P.$$

As we shall see, this oversimplifies what is actually the case, but it is a reasonable place from which to start.

Harry Gold, a clinical pharmacologist, recognized that the scientific evaluation of a treatment could not be achieved solely by anecdotal reports (Shapiro & Shapiro, 1997). Instead bona fide therapy must be proved to be superior to placebo. To accomplish this, Gold recommended that patients be assigned randomly to receive either the test drug (or procedure) or a placebo control. To exclude bias, he insisted that the participants in the trial be blinded, i.e., that neither the patient nor the investigators conducting the trial were to know what each group would receive. Patrick Wall (2000), an anesthesiologist, outlined the basic design of a randomized controlled clinical trial (RCT) as follows:

> A group of patients with some definite problem, e.g., a wisdom tooth extraction, are asked to volunteer for a trial. They are told that they will receive the new tablet (to relieve pain) or one that looks exactly the same. Then the patient, who does not know which tablet he received, tells an observer, who is also unaware of the nature of the tablet, whether the tablet reduced his pain. Finally after all the data has been collected, the code is broken and it is calculated whether the new drug is superior to placebo (p. 108).

The RCT design was accepted after it effectively demonstrated that streptomycin was more effective than placebo for the treatment of tuberculosis. It has remained the gold standard for evaluating new interventions ever since. In theory, the design of the RCT is sound, but in practice, problems have haunted it since its inception. For example, if a placebo control is not well chosen so that differences in the treatment groups become obvious to both patients and experimenters, this can negate the benefits of randomization and jeopardize the trial's interpretation. In addition, many interventions—including surgeries and a host of alternative or complementary therapies and psychotherapies—are not amenable either to randomization or blinding. Furthermore, subjects evaluated in RCTs are rarely representative of all of the types of patients who may eventually receive the treatment. Wall (2000) said the following:

No one should forget that the background for these trials is based on the powerful assumption that all people are the same and that individual psychosocial differences are irrelevant. This leads to the current vogue for "evidence-based medicine," driven partly by the tradition of academic medicine and partly by the financiers' need to identify a proven therapy whose cost is justified by trial (p. 108).

Despite these limitations, the RCT arguably remains the best method medical science has to offer for establishing the value of a new therapeutic intervention. However, with the advent of the RCT, placebo effects, which had previously been viewed either as the basis of medical therapeutics, or as the salutary results of interventions aimed at placating patients, became therapeutic confounders—factors to be accounted for in the statistical analysis of clinical experimentation (Harrington, 2002). This perspective on the placebo was at best neutral and at worst pejorative.

But if placebos are inert, one might expect that effective therapies would have little difficulty outperforming them. In practice, this is by no means the case. In an oft-quoted paper titled "The Powerful Placebo," Henry Beecher (1955; Figure 3.10), a Harvard University anesthesiologist, concluded that placebos were therapeutically effective for a wide variety of disorders approximately 35% of the time. In certain disorders (e.g., mild depression) placebo response rates in RCTs have in many instances been so high as to preclude establishing superiority for the drug being tested (Zimbroff, 2001).

The following example of an analysis of 117 RCTs comparing antacid medications with placebo underscores the issue (Lanza

Figure 3.10   Henry Beecher. Beecher, like Cabot, practiced at the Massachusetts General Hospital. His 1955 article "The Powerful Placebo" described many of the features of placebo effects. Together with Harry Gold, he helped to popularize the randomized clinical trial that is used today to evaluate the efficacy of a new drug or intervention.

et al., 1994). Two different antacids were compared to each other and to placebo for their ability to promote ulcer healing. Ulcer healing due to the placebo, as judged by an objective reduction in ulcer size, ranged from 0 to 100%, with a mean of $36 \pm 16\%$. The healing rate due to test drug ranged from 38 to 100%.

The test drugs in this study were statistically more effective than placebo, yet one might expect that a 35% mean placebo response rate requires an explanation. Recall that this is the mean response rate, so that an undisclosed number of patients receiving placebo actually developed better responses than those receiving the test antacids. Is this typical of the results in RCTs? The answer is yes. But as we have already seen, the RCT is not concerned with individual responses or with mechanisms of action; its purpose is simply to determine whether the test intervention is statistically superior to placebo.

Statistics are best applied to the analysis of large populations. It is not a method that can be directed at individuals or accurately applied to small groups. The RCT was specifically developed to avoid having to rely on anecdotal observations of one or a few patients. But when a physician quotes statistics concerning treatment options for an illness, the question that a given patient wants answered is, "How is this therapy going to affect me?" Based on how drugs are evaluated in a RCT, there is no definite answer. How a patient will respond will ultimately depend on whether or not he or she shares innumerable elements in common with responders. But what if the patient is more like those subjects whose response to the drug was less than placebo? In some cases, the chances of that being the case may be high. Fortunately, even if the patient does not respond to the drug, he or she may still be a candidate for developing a placebo response.

Are Placebo Effects Limited?

Some physicians are under the misconception that placebo effects are transient and minimal. Scientists tend to believe that interventions without a known mechanistic basis cannot yield impressive effects. But this is untrue, as both extraordinary and long-lived placebo effects have been reported. Consider the following study in which normal blood vessels were used to resupply the heart in patients who had coronary artery blockages. Bilateral internal mammary artery ligation was believed to reroute blood from the internal mammary arteries toward the heart, thereby increasing the myocardial blood supply blocked in angina.

It was an eminently sensible idea that worked as predicted— that is, until it was directly compared to sham placebo surgery. Subsequently, in two separate studies, chest incisions and exposure of the internal mammary arteries without ligation—a sham surgery that should have yielded no physiological change— proved to be as effective as the completed procedure in reducing both the frequency and severity of chest pain (Cobb et al., 1959; Dimond, Kittle, & Crockett, 1960). As might be expected, this promising surgical approach quickly fell out of favor.

Today, coronary artery bypass grafting and angioplasties are routinely performed for the treatment of angina. In these procedures, coronary artery blockages are, respectively, either bypassed or recanalized by instrumentation. They are common procedures, and most patients show a reduction in chest pain, improved blood flow documented by angiography, and increased pumping capacity by the heart. These changes must be due to the surgeries—or must they? By this point, the reader should be wary, having now seen two examples in which apparently effective surgeries were unable to outperform placebo.

To conduct the sham placebo trial, a patient with blocked coronary arteries would have to go through an extensive surgical procedure. In the 1950s and 1960s, when the internal mammary ligation procedure was evaluated, this was still possible, although there were reservations concerning the ethics of exposing a patient to the potentially harmful complications of an invasive sham surgery. Today, at least in the United States, there is likely no internal review board that would approve such a study. Increased ethical constraints have made it virtually impossible to examine many treatments critically. Until the current procedures are directly compared in an RCT, whether they are actually superior to placebo will remain uncertain.

It would appear that placebos can yield major effects, but is it possible that they actually act magically without a scientific mechanism? Such a conclusion holds little attraction for the rational minded. Alternatively, the mechanisms underlying the placebo response must exist but have not yet been discovered. This sounds more reasonable, but why then has medical science not addressed this issue more vigorously?

Why Has Medical Science Ignored the Placebo Response?

Despite the fact that placebo effects have been reported in the treatment of virtually all diseases and closely mimic those of active drugs and surgeries, little attention has been paid to why placebo effects occur at all. When important questions go unaddressed and unanswered, there is usually a reason. As will be discussed, placebo responses have been ignored for economic, psychological, and philosophical reasons. Let us begin with economics.

In her book *The Truth About the Drug Companies*, Marcia Angell (2004), former editor of the *New England Journal of Medicine*, expounded on the enormous influence that the pharmaceutical industry exerts on the current practice of medicine. Today pharmaceutical company representatives can be found roaming the corridors of most medical departments. The increased level of collaboration between academic medicine and the pharmaceutical industry appears to have begun in earnest during the 1980s, and it has increased progressively ever since. Pharmaceutical companies fund the RCTs in which new drugs are tested; they select physicians to conduct these trials; they contribute to their salaries; they reimburse them as consultants.* In addition, they provide medical residents and staff with innumerable perks that include dinners, trips, textbooks, food, pens, etc. The pharmaceutical industry copartners with medical schools in supporting basic research, often making large grants that attract new researchers and additional federal funds.

---

* Thanks to recent legislation, the pharmaceutical industry has also become a major funding source of the U.S. Federal Drug Administration through fees paid, thereby raising new conflicts of interest with respect to the rapid approval of new drugs.

From one perspective, these activities are admirable. They are certainly attractive if you happen to be a hospital or medical school administrator or one of the physicians on the receiving end of these favors. But what is too conveniently overlooked is that this relationship represents a serious conflict of interest—note that I am purposefully choosing not to term this a *potential* conflict of interest—particularly for the clinicians conducting the RCTs, as there is an unquestionably biased party supporting both their research and their salaries. Some academic physicians have argued that they are capable of maintaining their scientific objectivity separate from their financial interests, but this is disingenuous or at best naive. At a minimum, it is unconvincing.

Does this bear on why research into the science of the placebo response has been ignored? The answer is certainly yes. The pharmaceutical industry invests many millions of dollars in the development of a new drug; it is quite a large investment. Recouping their investment and making a profit ultimately depends on receiving approval to market the drug from the U.S. Federal Drug Administration. Few factors can potentially interfere more with a drug's ultimate approval than a high rate of competing placebo effects in the evaluative clinical trials, as they make it exceedingly difficult to establish statistically significant efficacy for a new drug.

Consequently, the pharmaceutical companies express very little interest in helping to establish what might be beneficial about placebo effects. However, they do occasionally exhibit interest in finding new ways to exclude placebo responders from their drug trials. A recent *Wall Street Journal* article reported on the efforts of "Big Pharma" to exclude placebo responders from clinical trials (Aboud, 2004). As journalist Jacky Law (2006) described in her monograph *Big Pharma*:

> Two companies, Lilly and Pfizer have therefore stumped up $1 mil-
> lion (not a lot of money in the scheme of things) to fund scientists at
> the University of California, Los Angeles (UCLA) to investigate how
> people who respond most to placebos might be isolated, although as
> will be shown, this is likely an ill-conceived strategy.… Selective strate-
> gies are high up pharma's agenda for all sorts of reasons that are to do
> with convenience and efficiency for the companies and, by definition
> have the effect of making medicines less applicable to the very people
> that they are designed to treat (p. 70).

But money is not everything, and there are other important reasons that scientists have ignored researching the placebo response.

Is It Placebo or Not?

Beecher's (1955) article was instrumental in establishing the scope of placebo effects. But when this classical report of placebo effects was recently reanalyzed, researchers concluded that the original study had failed to establish incontrovertible evidence for attributing the observed therapeutic effects as to placebos (Kienle & Kiene, 1997). Prior to the development of RCTs, clinical experimentation was virtually nonexistent, and placebo effects were identified in the daily practice of medicine. But how does one *know* whether therapeutic effects, occurring in response to the administration of a placebo, are placebo effects and not the result of other overlooked factors? This is a very difficult question to which there may not be a clear answer.

As Dylan Evans (2004) noted in *Placebo*, "All of the supposed demonstrations of the placebo effect on which the hyperbolic claims are based turn out to embody the same flaws that belied Beecher's paper. Whenever people in the placebo arm of a clinical trial get better, they assume that this improvement is entirely due to placebo without consideration of the other possible causes" (p. 13). We have encountered this issue before. But what Evans and others often neglect to consider is that neither the active nor the placebo arm of a clinical trial is designed to determine causation. They merely compare one group with another with respect to their potency.

When we argue about causation, we are guilty of the error that Hume (1888) warned against. Placebos by definition produce no *specific* effects, which means that nothing can help an investigator to establish directly what is a placebo effect. One either terms all of the therapeutic effects in the placebo arm of a trial *placebo effects* once all other possible contributions have been excluded. Of course, the same rationale must apply to the therapeutic effects that are observed in response to the drug or intervention being evaluated. But, as Hume suggested, we simply cannot be certain as to what causes the observed effects. This is a good reason to determine directly what a placebo response actually is because, until then, researchers must continue to wonder whether all other factors that might mimic placebo effects have been excluded, which frankly is impossible. The more scientific rigor one applies, the murkier matters become, and medical therapeutics cannot afford to become bogged down in philosophical debates.

Placebo Effects Versus the Natural History of Disease

Epidemiologists and biostatisticians are especially concerned with excluding confounding factors in the design and analysis of clinical trials. For this reason they are often skeptical concerning placebo effects. One common confounding factor is the natural tendency of symptoms to wax and wane, which is especially true of chronic disorders, as patients report having good and bad days with respect to their symptoms. Medical essayist Oliver Wendell Holmes (1860) summarized this phenomenon as follows:

> In the natural course of things some thousands of persons must be getting well or better of slight attacks of cold, rheumatic pains, every week in this city [Boston] alone. Hundreds of them do something or other in the form of remedy … and the last thing they do gets the credit of recovery (p. 193).

An undetermined percentage of therapeutic responses occur in patients who have received no treatment. One can control for this by adding a third group to an RCT that receives no treatment to control for placebo effects. Claude Bernard (1957) addressed this issue in his *Introduction to the Study of Experimental Medicine*:

> A physician who tries a remedy and cures his patient is inclined to believe that the cure is due to his treatment. But the first thing to ask is whether they have tried doing nothing ... for how can they otherwise know whether the remedy or nothing cured them?

However, this clinical trial design requires exceedingly large numbers of subjects if significance is to be established between groups. In 1994, fewer than 4% of clinical trials included both placebo and no-treatment arms (Ernst & Resch, 1995). So, it appears that most clinical trials are inadequately designed. Placebo effects observed in anecdotal situations are even more suspect. Additional confounders may include, for example, observer and subject biases, as well as effects that are attributable to a constituent of the placebo, such as a reaction to a dye product in a placebo pill.

Confounding Placebo: What Does It Mean to Regress to the Mean?

Another factor may be overlooked by nonstatisticians: *Regression to the mean* refers to the tendency of repeated measurements to drift from early values to an average center of distribution. Sir Francis Galton (1886) described what he termed "regression to mediocrity." In a series of experiments on the produce of seeds of different size but of the same species, Galton noted that offspring seeds tended to be larger than the parents when the parents were small, and smaller when the parents were large. He concluded that the greater the difference in the size of the parental seeds from the mean of the species, the larger the variance between parent and offspring. This phenomenon is not limited to plants; it is exhibited by virtually any biological variable (e.g., blood pressure, heart rate, plasma glucose). With multiple determinations, any value that deviates from the mean in the absence of disease will tend to regress toward it.

Consider the following example. Let us say that a new clinical trial seeks to recruit patients with blood pressures greater than 160/95 mm Hg and to exclude those with lower values. When John Doe is examined, his blood pressure of 170/96 mm Hg qualifies him for the study. But when he returns one week later, his blood pressure is now 150/90 mm Hg, so that he no longer meets the criterion for participation. What has occurred? There are multiple possible explanations. John Doe could have *white-coat hypertension,* a term used to describe elevated blood pressure caused by the anxiety of being examined by a health professional (O'Brien, 1999). Perhaps on his return visit, he was no longer fearful of the situation, and his blood pressure fell. A stressful life situation may have resolved between visits, and, as a consequence, his blood pressure was lower. Or he might have eaten a salty meal prior to the first measurement, which caused him to retain water that increased his blood pressure. But after these causes have been excluded, the most likely explanation is that Mr. Doe's blood pressure is simply obeying the statistical rule of regression to the mean.

For this reason, well-designed clinical trials always require multiple determinations of the variable to be tested prior to formally recruiting subjects. If this is not done, it is easy to mistake regression to the mean as a placebo effect. For example, had John Doe been recruited to the trial, randomized to the placebo group, and treated, his response would have been scored as a placebo effect. How often is this an issue? The fact is that it is impossible to be certain.* However, Clarence Davis (2002), a biostatistician from the University of North Carolina School of Public Health, offered the following educated guess:

> Regression to the mean is a possible explanation for many reported instances of placebo effect. However, I do not believe that regression to the mean can explain all reported placebo effects. Nevertheless, any research designed to measure placebo effects must carefully consider how regression to the mean might influence the results (p.165).

Therapeutics increasingly begins to resemble a shell game; with therapeutic effects not necessarily what they appear to be (Table 3.2). Even with rigorous controls, doubt persists, so one can imagine how an epidemiologist or statistician might bristle when claims are made for placebo effects in an anecdotal setting. It is also now apparent why our earlier accounting for therapeutic

---

* The reader might recall the earlier reference to the difference between an experiment in the physical sciences in which experiments are carried out multiple times, thereby reducing the influence of regression to the mean, and clinical trial investigation, in which this is not feasible.

Table 3.2 Factors That Can Contribute to Observed Therapeutic Effects

Specific activity of drug or intervention
Natural history of disease
Bias
Regression to mean
Adulterated drug
Placebo effect

effects was too simple. A more accurate reckoning must include not only (1) the effects due to the intervention (T_M) and (2) placebo effects (T_P) but also (3) regression to the mean (T_R) and sundry other (4) confounders (T_C) that I am lumping together mostly out of exasperation, so that

$$T_E = T_M + T_p + T_R + T_C.$$

Clearly, the business of accounting for therapeutic effect is not straightforward.

4 Placebo Effects—Who Gets Them?

Health that mocks the doctor's rules, knowledge never
learned of schools.

John Greenleaf Whittier

Introduction

For years, it was assumed that certain types of patients were
prone to developing placebo effects. During the 1960s and 1970s,
investigators attempted to determine the personality traits that
distinguished placebo responders. Arthur Shapiro, a psychiatrist
at the New York Hospital–Cornell University, devoted his career
to investigating placebo responses. In one large study, he examined 753 patients at the Payne Whitney Psychiatric Clinic who
were suffering from anxiety and depression (Shapiro & Shapiro, 1997). Patients were asked to express their preferences for
receiving psychotherapy, medication, or both. Interviews were
conducted and a variety of psychological questionnaires were
administered to determine which factors might predict placebo

responses. Subsequently, the subjects received a placebo capsule and were asked to rate their level of symptom relief.

Subjects who received both medication and psychotherapy had higher rates of placebo effects. Expectation that the placebo might represent a sedative-tranquilizer also yielded greater symptom relief. Subjects who deferred to their physician's decision as to which mode of treatment would likely be most efficacious reported improvement, as did those who expressed a positive attitude towards their doctor. Interestingly, the converse was not true, and it did not seem to matter if the doctor was positively inclined toward the patient or not. Finally, levels of both chronic anxiety and depression independently predicted placebo responses. Shapiro and Shapiro (1997) emphasized the importance of the following ancillary nonspecific factors:

> ... We believe that our results may be attributed to our having maximized, in the setting of our therapeutic studies, non-specific factors tending to favor positive expectations in the patient. These factors include giving patients an appointment within the week, conducting a comprehensive evaluation, using efficient procedures, seeing patients punctually at the appointed time, offering a pleasant atmosphere at a prestigious psychiatric clinic, using experienced research assistant and psychiatrists who were both drug-oriented and psychodynamically oriented, and using staff members who were interested in the specific drugs being tested, as well as in the non-specific or placebo effects of treatment. To enhance positive therapeutic outcome, therefore, treatment should include, at a minimum, these non-specific factors (p. 113).

But what was most informative about these results was their inability to demonstrate any predictive features with respect to personality and the development of placebo effects. Shapiro and Shapiro (1997) summarized the findings of the study as follows:

> It is commonly assumed that ... placebo reactors are less intelligent, less educated, more neurotic or psychotic, more frequently female, from lower social classes, more dependent, more inadequate, immature, impulsive, atypical, depressed, religious, stereotypic, more likely to have symptoms of hypochondriasis, obsessive compulsiveness, anger-hostility, bewilderment-confusion, and performance difficulties. In our studies and others there appear to be no consistent data relating these variables or demographic variables such as age, sex, intelligence, race, social class, ethnicity, religiosity, or religious background to placebo reaction (p. 117).

Despite long-standing beliefs to the contrary, no specific personality traits distinguished placebo responders from nonresponders; rather, what was important was the context created by the caregivers.

The Importance of Trait Versus State in Generating Placebo Effects

To appreciate the implications of Shapiro and Shapiro's (1997) findings, it is important to differentiate the parameters of *trait* and *state*. Psychologists define *trait* as a behavior that is reproducible over time. *State,* on the other hand, represents a behavior exhibited over relatively brief intervals and dependent primarily on conditions. For example, a person may be viewed generally as outgoing and friendly; however, when ill, he or she may unexpectedly become abrupt in dealing with others. The former is trait behavior; the latter is state behavior.

Consider the following example of how state affects placebo responses. In a study conducted in the 1950s, Wolf and Pinsky (1954) administered ipecac to healthy subjects on two occasions. Ipecac is an ancient remedy used to induce vomiting, such as in a patient who has inadvertently ingested a toxic substance. Following the ipecac, all of the subjects in the study became nauseated, and most vomited. Subsequently, the ipecac was administered again, but this time with a placebo pill and with the suggestion that the pill would potently inhibit vomiting.

The experiment was repeated several times. All of the 23 healthy subjects developed a placebo response at least once; however, there was no way to predict whether the response might occur on subsequent occasions for the same patients, as they responded differently at different times. The placebo responses were dependent on the specific conditions or context created by experimenters. These findings suggest that most subjects have the capacity to develop placebo effects and that placebo responses are state, not trait, behaviors.

The Importance of the Caregiver in Determining Placebo Responses

A number of studies have attempted to resolve whether the attitudes of caregivers can influence the likelihood of developing placebo effects. W. R. Houston (1938), in a paper titled "Doctor

Himself as a Therapeutic Agent," reported that the behavior of the physician was an important factor in therapeutic outcomes. K. B. Thomas (1994) showed that the chances of developing a positive therapeutic outcome were increased when patients viewed their physician as optimistic, experienced, and competent. Conversely, physician skepticism tended to reduce therapeutic benefits.

The attention paid to a patient may be an important determinant of placebo effects and therapeutic outcome. Thomas (1987) demonstrated that the number of visits with health-care professionals was the most significant factor in predicting placebo responses. He also concluded that many patients in the primary-care setting show improvements in their symptoms after meeting with a physician, even in the absence of a specific therapeutic intervention. Psychiatrists have long recognized the importance of exhibiting concerned attention toward patients. Michael Balint (1972), a psychoanalyst, championed the idea of introducing psychoanalytical techniques into the delivery of primary medical care. He summarized the state of medical practice as follows:

> Nowadays with more and more of us becoming isolated and lonely, people have hardly anyone to whom they can take their troubles. It is undeniable that fewer and fewer people take them to their priests. The only person who is available … is the doctor. In many people, emotional stress is accompanied by or tantamount to bodily sensations. So they come to their doctor and complain (p. 225).

As physicians are inclined increasingly to limit their role exclusively to their subspecialty interest, psychological needs are relegated to ancillary members of the health team. Patients who require substantial personal attention may find themselves referred to a consulting psychiatrist or to the hospital social worker. But as Shorter (1985) pointed out, approximately 63% of patients with anxiety or depression, with or without physical symptoms, approach their family doctors for treatment and do not wish to see another health-care worker.

The compartmentalization of care is a cause of considerable unhappiness among patients. Disenchanted with the impersonal nature of the modern medical dynamic and unable to elicit the attention that they require, some have chosen to abandon traditional medicine altogether to seek out alternative modes of treatment (Eisenberg et al., 1998). These patients may be well justified in their choice, as when Lin et al. (2001) examined patient satisfaction based on time spent with their physician, they found that the average consultation with a family doctor in the United States lasted only 11 minutes. Contrast this with a 30-minute on average period of patient contact in homeopathic practice.

The brevity of contact in traditional medicine is hardly sufficient for patients to communicate a primary complaint, let alone to establish anything that might pass for a relationship. It is certainly not conducive to eliciting a placebo response. From what is increasingly being gleaned from the field of evolutionary psychology, a patient's desire to be pampered may be motivated purposely to elicit from caregivers what is required to evoke a placebo response.

Is Psychotherapy a Placebo?

Some researchers have questioned whether the beneficial effects of psychotherapy might be due to the placebo response. This possibility is suggested by the scarcity of evidence that one mode of psychotherapy is more effective than any other (Luborsky, Singer, & Luborsky, 1975). In a meta-analysis of 25,000 patients treated with 78 modes of psychotherapy, no therapeutic benefits were specifically attributable to the method of psychotherapy, therapeutic setting, duration of treatment, types of patients, or the training of the therapists (Smith, Glass, & Miller, 1980). Whereas the authors of this study did conclude that psychotherapy is more effective than placebo, their conclusion has by no means been generally accepted.

It is understandable that psychoanalysts who have trained for many years might choose to reject the idea that their therapeutic success is attributable to the placebo response, so when that possibility was specifically raised, most did dismiss the notion (Shapiro & Shapiro, 1997). But psychotherapist B. J. Cohen (2003) in *The Theory and Practice of Psychiatry* noted that all types of psychotherapy share certain features in common. These include a confidential relationship with another person that takes place in a secure setting, a rational theme that assists in the construction of meaning for the patient's distress, and a ritual procedure aimed at restoring the patient's health. Compare this list with the ancient Asklepian rites, and it is easy to conclude that psychotherapy shares a great deal in common with placebo treatment.

Stevens, Hynan, and Allen (2000) conducted a meta-analysis of 80 psychotherapeutic studies published in the literature. They examined differences between the effects of so-called common factors and specific treatment with respect to well-being, symptoms, and activities of daily living. They demonstrated that putative placebo effects contributed to improvements in symptoms and life activities, although they also concluded that specific therapies were more effective.

In *The Illusion of Psychotherapy*, W. M. Epstein 1995. p. 130 skeptically concluded, "Proof that psychotherapy adds little to common human kindness or to simple social activities ... that it may be in essence little more than a placebo response invalidates the professional utility of that field." However, as psychiatrist Arthur Kleinman (1988) suggested, if psychotherapy is nothing more than a mode of maximizing the placebo response, then "it should be applauded rather than condemned for exploiting a useful therapeutic process which is underutilized in health care" (p. 112). From the perspective of the present discussion, Kleinman is on target, and we shall soon see why. Whether psychotherapy is a placebo intervention cannot be definitively answered here. But there can be no doubt that psychological factors contribute to the development of placebo effects.

How Expectancy Influences Placebo Responses

Albert Bandura (1997), a research psychologist, proposed expectancy as a critical factor in all therapeutic responses, and Irving Kirsch, a placebo scientist, has demonstrated repeatedly that expectancy is a major determinant of placebo effects (e.g., Kirsch & Weixel, 1988). In one study, subjects were divided into two groups and given either caffeinated or decaffeinated coffee to drink. Neither the subjects nor the experimenters knew which they would receive. Another group was told that they would receive caffeinated coffee but instead was given a decaffeinated brand. At 20 minutes, the group that had been deceived showed significantly higher systolic blood pressures and evidence of physiologic arousal, both changes that would be expected from ingesting caffeine. This experiment demonstrates that objective physiological effects can be reversed by psychological expectations that counter the objective truth of the experimental conditions, comparable to what Wolf and Pinsky (1954) demonstrated in their placebo experiments with the ingestion of ipecac.

Many of these placebo experiments feature a trickster quality. But expectancy is serious business. Antidepressant drugs are thought to act by altering levels of brain neurotransmitters; however, it takes several weeks before these changes can be measured. Yet patients may report symptomatic relief within hours or days of receiving an antidepressant. For this reason, it should come as little surprise that some general practitioners choose to prescribe psychoactive medications in schedules that are theoretically sub-optimal while continuing to observe beneficial responses. As Kessel (1973 p. 243) noted, "These agents are often used in very small doses as ... stock placebos. 'Librium' has virtually replaced liniment."

Recognizing the importance of placebo effects in the treatment of depression, Sapirstein and Kirsch (1996) conducted a meta-analysis of 3,000 patients who received either antidepressant medication, psychotherapy, placebo, or no treatment. They found that 27% of therapeutic responses were attributable to drug activities, 50% to psychological factors surrounding the administration of drug, and 23% to nonspecific factors. In other words, 73% of the response to the drug was unrelated to its pharmacological activities. Subsequently, these researchers suggested that the efficacy of antidepressant medications might be primarily attributable to expectancies enhanced by nonspecific physical sensations induced by the medication. In other words, antidepressants may actually be no better or specific than placebos. As Law (2006) pointed out with respect to the difficulties in separating out antidepressant from placebo effects, "The clinical difference is not that impressive-and it is getting worse." She added that Timothy Walsh, a psychiatrist at Columbia University, confirms the following:

> A higher percentage of depressed patients get better on placebos than 20 years ago.... This is largely due to rising expectations from the public about what drugs can do, providing yet another illustration of

the exquisite expectation-management corner pharma has driven itself into (p. 70).

The Early Response Rates in Clinical Trials: A Classical Placebo Effect

It is well recognized in clinical medicine that the early response rates to new treatments are often higher than at later times (Moerman, 2002). There are many potential explanations for this phenomenon, but expectancy is certainly one of them. As enthusiasm for a novel experimental approach is tempered by reports of therapeutic failures, the expectations of both subjects and the experimenters tend to diminish. Many initially promising therapeutic approaches ultimately do not stand the test of time.

Psychologist Bruno Klopfer (1957) offered an extraordinary example of this phenomenon. A patient with advanced lymphoma, a malignancy of the lymph glands, was enrolled in an experimental chemotherapy trial with krebiozen, a new agent. His tumor evaporated in response to the treatment, and both he and the research clinicians were understandably elated. But when results began to eke out from other centers showing that the drug was ineffective, he rapidly relapsed. His doctors, suspecting that his initial response may have been a placebo effect, told him that they had a new double-strength version of krebiozen but instead injected him with saline. He again had an excellent response. Unfortunately, when it was ultimately reported that krebiozen was ineffective, this patient's tumor rapidly recurred, and he died.

Recently, a novel chemotherapeutic agent called gefitinib (Iressa) has been reported to produce dramatic tumor reduction in some patients with lung cancer (Lynch et al., 2004). The effects of this agent have been attributed to its specific effects on the epidermal growth factor receptor, a protein expressed by a subset of lung cancers that plays a role in tumor proliferation. The specific antitumor responses to this drug were widely publicized by an article published in the *New England Journal of Medicine*, in which they were lauded as a scientific breakthrough in the designer treatment of cancer. This report spurred a rash of molecular testing to determine whether patients' tumors express the epidermal growth factor receptor that reportedly responded to the drug. But at the same time this research was being reported, the drug manufacturer was considering withdrawing the drug from the market due its limited beneficial effects in most clinical trials. Whether Iressa ultimately proves to be beneficial is uncertain. It may well act specifically on a small subset of patients, but as more patients are examined the results do not appear to be robust, and it is entirely possible that the early reports of responses were placebo effects. A recent statement by the U.S. Federal Drug Administration (FDA 2005) on the benefits of Iressa suggests that the initial enthusiasm was overrated:

> The FDA has announced revisions to the label of the antineoplastic gefitinib (Iressa).... Postmarketing studies have shown that, unlike

other drugs, gefitinib doesn't make patients with this type of cancer live longer.... AstraZeneca will limit the availability of the drug....

Meaning and Placebo Effects

Precise definitions of mental states are difficult. In an effort to operationalize thoughts, affects, and behaviors in order to analyze them scientifically, cognitive and behavioral scientists have tended to create definitions that can seem artificial. Understandably, one might be confused about the fine distinctions among expectancy, hope, beliefs, and meaning—all of which have been suggested as determinants of the placebo response. Daniel Moerman (2002), a medical anthropologist, has stressed the importance of meaning in his studies of the placebo response. To Moerman, meaning is so critical a determinant of placebo effects that he has suggested that the term *meaning response* replace *placebo response* in the literature. He has also opined that the idea that placebos are inert simply does not accord with their efficacy in practice and should be abandoned.

Moerman (2002) cited compelling evidence from a variety of studies to support his viewpoints. For example, in a study conducted by Montgomery and Kirsch (1996), subjects were given an inert colored liquid that contained thyme and water in a bottle labeled "Trivaricaine: Approved for Research Purposes Only." *Trivaricaine* is a formidable-sounding term that sounds like Novocain, a widely known anesthetic. But Trivaricaine does not exist; it is merely a concocted name. The subjects were pretreated topically with this solution and then were subjected to a series of painful stimuli; subsequently, they were asked to rate their level of pain. Based on their perceived meaning (expectation/belief?) of the experimental conditions, the subjects routinely reported less pain in areas pretreated with the solution labeled Trivaricaine.

Howard Brody, a family practitioner with long-standing interest in placebo research, has proposed that an important feature of medical diagnosis is that it supplies patients with meaning for their symptoms (e.g., Brody & Brody, 2000). Diagnosis is part of a larger category of therapeutic meaning and as such may contribute to placebo effects.

Products and Placebos

Up until now, we have focused on salutary placebo effects. But negative placebo, or *nocebo,* responses are also common. The ultimate nocebo response was reported by Harvard physiologist Walter Cannon (1942; Figure 4.1) as *voodoo death,* an extraordinary phenomenon in which an adept of the voudon religion actually dies from fear in reaction to having been cursed. On a more mundane level, a commonly encountered nocebo effect results from reading the inserts of drug packages that list, at times in distressing detail, the potential side effects of a medication. Most physicians are well acquainted with patients who, after receiving a new prescription, inquire skeptically about one or more of its potential side effects that they have read about. In my experience,

Figure 4.1 Walter Cannon. Cannon was a renowned physiologist at the Harvard Medical School. His research included elucidating the physiology of stress. His report of "voodoo death" is the ultimate example of a nocebo effect.

reassurance does little to assuage these concerns, and most patients will report stopping the drug as a result of having developed the very side effects that concerned them. Expectation also affects how patients respond to the route of drug delivery. Most patients are aware that strong medicines are delivered by injection, so it is little surprise that placebos administered by injection also prove more potent than those given orally, in support of the widely held belief, "No pain, no gain."

At times, placebo effects are elicited by minor details of the therapeutic encounter (Moerman, 2002). For example, the frequent administration and larger pills both yield greater placebo effects. The colors of pills can also affect responses, with blue pills tending to soothe symptoms and red pills exciting them. This presumably reflects the conventional idea that blue is a cool color, whereas red is a hot one. Perhaps Viagra, the "little blue pill," should have instead been packaged as a large red one, but here it appears that pharmaceutical companies uncharacteristically opted for understatement.

The branding of medications is a definite determinant of the magnitude of placebo effects. A well-known proprietary brand name can evoke a more potent response than generic brand X for patients who believe they can trust a specific brand. And they would be correct—but not because of what is actually in the pill. For this reason, it is generally unwise to overrule a patient's stated preference for a nongeneric drug, because the generic may prove ineffective or may not be tolerated.

Cultural, societal, and religious differences also contribute to how meaning is constructed. For example, a medical scientist and a Christian Scientist will attribute different meanings to healing. Meaning is often shared in common within communities and families. However, personal experiences, memories, and emotional coloring can lead to idiosyncratic perspectives. For these reasons, it is difficult to predict how a given patient is likely to construe the therapeutic encounter.

The arguments that support the role of meaning in producing placebo effects are compelling. There is little doubt that how meaning is construed from the context of the therapeutic encounter is a major determinant of whether, and to what extent, placebo effects will develop. But, the term *meaning response* does little to explain how placebos act. It fails to explain precisely how a psychological construct like *meaning* mediates changes in somatic physiology. Furthermore, it lacks precision, as, one begins to inquire specifically as, what is actually meant by *meaning* or attempts to distinguish it from expectancy, faith, belief, or hope, discerning the answer may be difficult. The placebo response demands its own mechanistic exegesis.

5 What Do We Know About How Placebos Act?

A drowsy numbness pains my sense, as though of hemlock I had drunk, or emptied some dull opiate to the drains.

John Keats

Introduction

To date, most research into placebos action has centered on models in which pain is modulated by the administration of a placebo. Two pathways have received considerable attention. One is behavioral conditioning, which is based on how responses to therapeutic interventions are learned and recalled in response to placebo administration. The other is the opioid pathway, in which the endogenous release of opioids has been implicated as a cause of placebo analgesia. Obviously, there is potential for considerable overlap, as the behavioral model is a psychological response, whereas the opioid model is a biochemical one.

Conditioning and Placebo Effects

Russian scientist Ivan Pavlov (Figure 5.1) demonstrated that psychic reflexes could influence the autonomic activities of dogs. In his most famous experiment, the sight of food, an unconditioned stimulus (UCS), led to increased salivation by a dog. When the sight of food was repeatedly coupled to the sound of a bell, the conditioned stimulus (CS), the sound of the bell, was

Figure 5.1   Ivan Pavlov. A Russian scientist, Pavlov discovered that behaviors could be conditioned via his experiments with dogs. Behavioral conditioning continues to be considered as an explanatory mechanism of the placebo response.

by itself eventually able to produce salivation, i.e., a conditioned response (CR). The core stratagem of behavioral conditioning can be generically described as follows. A neutral CS is coupled to a biological UCS, and with repetition, a novel CR develops to the CS. The conditioning model is an excellent example of how the mind–brain automatically and insistently constructs causality. The neutral CS is interpreted by the mind–brain as linked to the UCS—that is, as causal. In fact, there may be no connection other than temporal proximity, but as Hume (1888) recognized, the mind–brain fails to discern this.

Laboratory animals can be conditioned in a variety of different ways, and there is a huge literature concerning conditioned behavior. However, it was not widely appreciated until recently that the nervous system could also be conditioned to yield activities outside of itself. In the 1970s, Robert Ader and colleagues conducted a series of experiments demonstrating that when cyclophosphamide, a drug that antagonizes immune function, was coupled to the administration of saccharine in the drinking water of rats, immunosuppression could eventually be evoked by saccharine alone (Ader, 1997). Longo et al. (1999), immunologists at the National Cancer Institute, demonstrated that when human macrophages were activated by a potent cytokine, interferon-gamma, together with a placebo, in time the conditioned response to placebo led to effective activation in its own right.

In other experiments, patients with asthma were exposed to the aroma of vanilla together with medications that could dilate their constricted airways (Ley, 1995). With conditioning, the bronchodilator response was evoked by the aroma of vanilla alone. Remarkable experiments like these suggested that there was greater integration between the nervous system and other organ systems than previously expected. If behavioral conditioning could influence immune reactivity and airways contraction, might it not also participate in the placebo response?

Placebo Response: All Too Human?

As *placebo response* is defined here, it is evoked exclusively by a therapeutic dynamic in man. But if it is the result of behavioral conditioning, and if conditioning can be demonstrated in laboratory animals, can other species also develop placebo effects? This was the reasoning behavioral scientist Robert Hernstein (1962) offered in a controversial article titled "Placebo Effects in the Rat." Perhaps unduly influenced by the radical behaviorist B. F. Skinner, Hernstein argued against the prevailing notion that placebo responses were dependent on symbolic thought—a subjective mental state that can not be observed—and also challenged the idea that they were somehow triggered by vague and subjective features of the relationship between patients and their doctors.

Aspects of Hernstein's (1962) argument are undoubtedly correct. Carefully designed placebo experiments with ethanol, nicotine, and a variety of drugs all support the idea that conditioning contributes to placebo effects. But the limitation of

Hernstein's argument is that although no clear distinctions may exist between how men and rats are conditioned, the repertoire of conditioned behaviors in man is more extensive and also includes mind–body states that can be activated by the doctor–patient relationship in order to yield placebo effects. The experiments of Leuchter et al. (2002) with positron emission tomography (PET) and functional magnetic resonance imaging (fMRI) scanning have convincingly demonstrated that previously nonobservable psychological states have objective and measurable neurological underpinnings. The black box of the mind has been opened—at least to some degree.

Models of behavioral conditioning do not formally require explanation by biological mechanisms any more than the laws of gravity require the discovery of gravitons to be useful and predictive. Yet science does value deeper levels of explanation. If analgesia can be conditioned, it stands to reason that there must be an underlying biological mechanism responsible for mediating pain relief.

Opioid Model: Placebos as Analgesia

Models of placebo analgesia are based on nonpharmacological stimuli that can alleviate pain, including the sight of a pill or syringe or the sound of a soothing voice. However, these behavioral cues do not explain how the perception of a painful stimulus can be physiologically diminished. Levine, Gordon, and Fields (1978) showed that placebo analgesia could be inhibited by pretreating subjects with the drug naloxone, which blocks morphine receptors on neurons in the brain. Price and Soerensen (2002) proposed that opiates—endogenous neurotransmitters released by the brain and recognized to reduce pain perception—also mediate placebo-induced analgesia.

The physiology of pain has been extensively investigated. Powerful suppression of pain perception occurs in rodents following electrical stimulation of the periaqueductal gray matter of the brainstem, an ancient area of the brain (Reynolds, 1969). Comparable results have been observed by the direct injection of opioids into this area (Takagi, Doi, & Akaiake, 1976). Opioid pathways in the brain are not localized; instead, they project to a variety of areas of the brain, including the amygdala, and several other distinct nuclei of the brainstem (Price & Soerensen, 2002). The wide distribution of opioid producing neurons has the advantage of integrating opioid release with neural pathways from diverse brain regions, exactly what one might expect to see in a conditioned response.

Endogenous opioid substances, including enkephalin, have been localized in areas of the brain responsible for mediating pain and analgesia as well as in neurons that express receptors for opioids on their cell membranes. Naloxone reverses electrically stimulated analgesia (Watkins & Mayer, 1982). Although these findings do not prove that opioids mediate placebo-induced analgesia, they provide compelling supportive evidence for the idea.

Of Mice and Men: Small Genetic Differences Yield Large Behavioral Ones

As these studies were conducted in laboratory animals, the question naturally arose as to whether they were also applicable to man. The genetic differences between mice and man are surprisingly limited. The mouse and human genomes are 99% identical. We know this, as both the human and murine genomes have been successfully cloned and their gene sequences painstakingly compared (Waterston et al., 2002). But this does not mean that men and mice are virtually identical. Rather, it suggests that even small genetic differences can yield complex differences at the level of physiological activity. Despite their similarities, there is good precedent for experimental models in mice not translating well into humans. Indeed, if they did, we would have eradicated a variety of disorders that can be reproducibly cured in mice but not in man, including many forms of cancer.

But in the case of placebo analgesia, the similarities between mice and man have been compelling. Comparative neuroanatomy demonstrated similar pain-related circuitry in the brainstem and spinal cord of all mammals, including man, suggesting that pain pathways are both ancient and highly conserved. In addition, neuroscientists showed that stimulating the human aqueductal gray matter of the brainstem effectively reduced intractable pain (Richardson & Akil, 1973). Endogenous opioids have also been identified in the human nervous system and electrical stimulation increases levels of potent analgesics (e.g., the endorphins).

As in the mouse, all of the required elements are present and accounted for.

Placebo Analgesia: Getting Down to Basics

In a series of elegant experiments, placebo researchers have been able to demonstrate that placebo analgesia is dependent on opioid pathways in man (Benedetti & Amanzio, 1997). Recently, researchers have extended these observations to include how conditioning, expectancy, and the opioid system cooperate in yielding placebo analgesia. In one experiment, subjects were told that a strong analgesic (i.e., placebo) cream, a weak cream (i.e., placebo), or a control cream would be applied to the forearm prior to a painful thermal skin stimulus (Price & Soerensen, 2002). First, the subjects were conditioned by combining the application of these creams with purposefully graded decrements in the painful stimulus. As a result, subjects reported strong, weak, or no reduction in their pain, respectively. When the level of stimulation was readjusted so that all subjects received the same stimulus strength, analgesia varied as expected based on prior conditioning. Placebo analgesia was also inhibited by naloxone, demonstrating its opioid dependence.

One important finding in these studies was that the placebo analgesia proved to be specifically limited to areas of the skin that had been treated. This implies that the placebo effects are not the result of a global response that would have extended to include uninvolved areas of skin. Instead, the neural pathways mediating the placebo analgesia were anatomically localized and specific and apparently either similar or identical to pathways that mediate nonplacebo responses to pain. As a result, one may conclude that placebo effects are neither imaginal (i.e., the result of purely mental activities) or imaginary (i.e., fictitious). Rather, they are objectively verifiable with specific pathways of action. They differ from an active analgesic drug only in how they are evoked.

Experiments like these have succeeded in linking the psychological elements of expectancy and meaning with conditioned responses and in rooting these responses in specific neural and molecular pathways. They demonstrate that mind–body placebo effects develop implicitly; that is, they are unconscious. But there is still a critical missing link. How does one get from a mental state of expectancy to pain relief? The elephant in the room is the mind–body problem, and if the placebo response is to be explained, it must be addressed.

A (Very) Brief Guided Tour of the Nervous System

Whereas progress has been made in the last two decades with respect to the mind–body problem, there is still much work to be done. In the next sections, a model for mind–body effects and the placebo response will be developed. Aspects of what will be proposed find direct support in observation, whereas others are more speculative. But first, it is necessary to examine briefly how the nervous system functions with emphasis on what is germane to mind–body interaction.

The basic unit of the nervous system is the neuron (Figure 5.2). It is a specialized cell with an excitable cell membrane that can generate, transmit, and receive impulses by transforming chemical and electrical impulses. Incoming afferent impulses are transmitted across microscopic gaps between adjacent neurons called synapses. Chemical neurotransmitters released by the presynaptic neuron can either excite or depress the postsynaptic neuron. When the postsynaptic neuron is sufficiently stimulated away from its resting potential, it generates an action potential that results in the release of preformed stores of neurotransmitter into the synapse that either activate or inhibit the adjacent

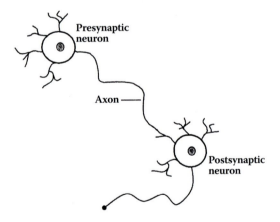

Figure 5.2 Neurons and synapse. The basic unit of the nervous system, activation of neurons leads to the transmission of impulses. The brain is a complex organ of highly connected neurons.

postsynaptic neuron. Whether a neuron develops an action potential is determined by the sum of depolarizing and hyperpolarizing influences at its cell surface membrane.

The estimated numbers of neuronal connections in the human brain is astronomical. Roughly, there are approximately 100 billion neurons and 1 million billion connections, a number of truly inconceivable magnitude. A single neuron can influence the behavior of upward of 10,000 other neurons (Figure 5.3). The behavior of neuronal circuitry is characterized by its capacity for feedback—that is, by the reentry of transmitted signals back to their source after modification by other neurons in the circuit. It has been estimated that no more than three orders of synaptic

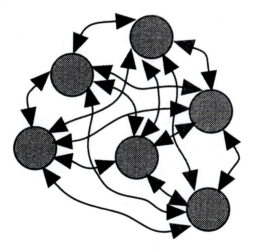

Figure 5.3 Interconnectedness of Neurons. The drawing indicates the extensive interconnectedness of neuronal networks and their capacity for reentry.

transmission occur in the brain before the original impulse is returned in modified form to its origin (Spitzer, 1999).

Specific neural behavior requires that some pathways be activated while others are inhibited. Small columns of activated neurons in the neocortex activate adjacent neurons while inhibiting distant competing pathways via a series of gamma-amino butyric acid (GABA)-secreting interneurons. This renders competition between adjacent neurons less effective. The result is a center-surround structure that results in selective advantage for the activated cortical column (Spillmann & Werner, 1990). The elimination of competing neural pathways is termed neuronal pruning, as it strengthens some pathways at the expense of others. With repeated stimulation deactivated pathways may actually drop out of the repertoire due to a lack of neurotrophic sustenance.

According to neuroscientist William Calvin, the unit of neuronal processing throughout the brain's neocortex is a hexagonal arrangement of neurons occupying approximately 0.5 mm of the cortex (Spitzer, 1999). These neuronal networks are comparable to what computational scientists have called neural nets. Computational neural nets mimic how the brain learns. They can rapidly solve problems relating to complex pattern recognition, the acquisition of syntactical skills, and other tasks typically associated with higher cortical brain functions.

The cerebral cortex—and in particular the frontal lobes— accounts for most of the increased size of the human brain

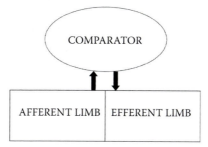

Figure 5.4   Servomotor System. The drawing shows the afferent, comparator, and efferent limbs of a servomotor mechanism.

compared with other species. The cerebral cortex mediates higher cortical functions of perception, thought, abstraction, and language. The cortex in turn modulates the activities of the lower brain centers via a top-down strategy. A dense network of reciprocal neuronal connections between the cortex and thalamus, the so-called thalamocortical circuitry, integrates sensory input both from outside and within the body. The summed effect leads to the higher cortical activity termed consciousness (Edelman & Tononi, 2000).

Other brain structures also play a critical role in mental activities. The limbic system—a loosely defined set of neuronal regions that includes the orbitofrontal cortex, anterior cingulated gyrus, amygdala, and hypothalamus—serves as an interface between higher and lower brain regions and contributes to the appraisal of meaning, social cognition, and emotion.

The hippocampus, located deep within the inner surface of the brain, is a critical element in learning, memory formation, and recollection. It is integrated with the limbic system so that memory and emotional experience are inextricably linked via the brain's hard wiring (Siegel, 1999).

Darwin and Neural Processing

A unique feature of the brain is its ability to respond rapidly and in a complex fashion to its environment. In engineering terms, the nervous system is a servomotor system that receives input from its surroundings, compares it to previously learned patterns, and then reacts to the informational input (Carver & Scheir, 1998; see Figure 5.5).

Learning about the environment begins in utero. Gerald Edelman (2003; Figure 5.6), an eminent neuroscientist and Nobel laureate, suggested that Charles Darwin's (Figure 5.7) principles of evolution apply not only to the phylogeny of the brain but also to its competing neural pathways in development. Edelman (1989) referred to the genetically determined blueprint of the brain as its primary neuronal repertoire. At birth, the primary repertoire includes excess numbers of neurons, a strategy that compensates for subsequent pruning and age-related neuron loss. Darwinian neural selection is a real time strategy adapted to meet environmental challenges. Darwinian competition is achieved by the selection of specific neural pathways that potentially confer biological advantage over competing pathways. Psychologist Donald Hebb (1949) suggested that learning was the direct result of strengthened synaptic connections between neurons. Experience-dependent activation

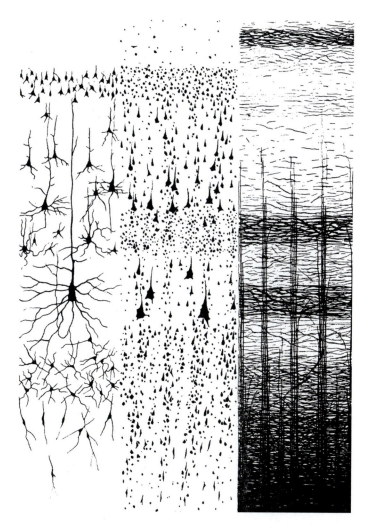

Figure 5.5 Columns of Cortical Neurons. The figure illustrates the columnar configuration of neurons in the cortex. Activated columns of neuronal columns inhibit the activities of adjacent columns, thereby enhancing their own selection.

Figure 5.6   Gerald Edelman. A neuroscientist and Nobel Laureate in immunology, Edelman's theory of neural Darwinism has revolutionized studies of consciousness. The model of the placebo response that is developed in this text owes much to Edelman's insights.

yields a secondary neuronal repertoire that is orders of magnitude more complex with respect to information-processing capacities than the primary repertoire (Edelman, 1989). The secondary repertoire reflects the history of an individual's nervous system interactions with the environment.

Neural Networks

Much of what we currently know concerning how the brain processes information has been gained from the study of computa-

Figure 5.7 Charles Darwin. British naturalist Darwin's theory of evolution has been applied as an explanatory model to virtually all aspects of human physiology and psychology. It is likely that the placebo response was selected for its adaptive effects.

tional neural nets (Spitzer, 1999). Neural nets are constructed based on relatively simple computational principles. A signal input is attributed a value or strength somewhere between 0 and 1, with 1 representing a signal capable of generating an action potential and 0 leading to no activity. The input is modified at the level of nodal synapses, so that it is either fully or partially transmitted or inhibited. This process is termed synaptic weight. The product of the individual inputs and their synaptic weights determines the output of the system. If the sum of these products is >1, the neuron will fire. But if it is between 0 and 1, the neuron will not generate an action potential. For real neurons, the threshold for activation is more nuanced and probabilistic, so rather than obeying a strict quantized step function it more closely approximates an S-shaped sigmoid curve.

Unlike standard computing strategies that solve problems by rapid computations in series, neural nets adopt a strategy of parallel and distributed information processing. The signals are distributed among connected nodal points within the computer program in much the same way that neurons are distributed within the brain. Like the brain, a computational neural net is characterized by reentry. The high interconnectivity of real neurons has led some to postulate that brain activities are the result of the summed output of the brain's entire neuronal repertoire. This domain-general model of brain activity is based on the observation that the entire brain is metabolically active at any given time. From this perspective, the brain is a large distributed parallel processor with no constraints on how it processes information. Alternatively, brain activities may be viewed as domain specific, meaning that their activities are compartmentalized into modules. These modules are informationally encapsulated so that other parts of the brain do not influence their core function.

Modular architecture requires fewer connections and learns faster than nonmodular systems (Rueckl, Cave, & Kosslyn, 1989). Most neuroanatomical and functional studies support the idea that the brain processes information primarily via domain-specific modules, although some domain-general processes may also participate (Kosslyn & Koenig, 1992).The importance of domain specificity will be revisited when a model of the placebo response is considered.

Memory

Memory provides the basis for how placebo responses develop. Psychologist Daniel Siegel (1999) suggested that memory can be defined as "the way that past events determine future behaviors" (p. 72). Edelman (1989) proposed that the essence of memory is the neural reconstruction of experience, much as psychoanalyst Sigmund Freud did at the turn of the last century with his concept of how memory is retranscribed (*nachtraglichkeit*) (Freud, 1914b).

Edelman (1989) evoked the Darwinian paradigm in suggesting that memories are retrievable precisely because they have an increased probability of being selected from among competing neural pathways. Practice strengthens neuronal connections, as any student studying for an examination will attest to. The probability of recalling what has been learned is a function of the strength of the neuronal connections of the encoded information. The adage "use it or lose it" applies to memory, although we are all aware that remote memories can persist over the course of a lifetime with little reinforcement. But in most instances, when the contents of these memories are examined they are vague.

However, some can remain poignant, as Marcel Proust (1993) illustrated in *In Search of Lost Time,* as visceral recollections of events of one's youth.

All memories are the recollection of what has previously been learned. Long-term potentiation (LTP) is a critical concept in memory research, as it helps to explain how memories are consolidated and stored (Kandel, Schwartz, & Fesell, 1991). A crucial element in LTP is the N-methyl-D-aspartate (NMDA) glutamate receptor (Bliss & Collingridge, 1993) that binds the excitatory neurotransmitter glutamate. The NMDA receptor functions as a molecular detector of concurrent events, strengthening synaptic connections between a strongly signaling presynaptic neuron and a postsynaptic neuron. Highly diffusible gases such as nitric oxide and carbon monoxide, released locally by the postsynaptic neuron, act in retrograde fashion to stimulate the presynaptic neuron, there by further strengthening their synaptic connection. This potentially can transform a weak synaptic connection into a strong one. This also promotes the likelihood of subsequent pathway selection and increases synaptic connectivity, which is the basis of behavioral conditioning.

Memory includes the processes of encoding, storage, and retrieval. But memory storage is a misnomer, as there is no area in the brain where memories are physically stored. For years scientists examined the brains of laboratory animals searching for memory traces, or engrams, within specific regions of the brain or in proteins and nucleic acids, where in theory they might have been encoded and stored. What they discovered instead was that it required the destruction of widely distributed parts of the brain to eradicate most memories. This is because memories are in fact stored only *in potentia*—that is, as a probabilistic capacity for activating specific neuronal pathways that may connect widely different areas of the brain.

Operationally, memory can be categorized in several ways. Memory can be explicit, meaning that one can consciously recall what has previously been learned. Alternatively, it can be implicit, or unconscious, and subject to retrieval without reliance on conscious recall. Explicit memory, in turn, may be subdivided into semantic and episodic memory. Semantic memory is the information that one tries to remember, such as when taking an exam. It includes previously learned names, dates, places, and ideas. It requires conscious attention both when new information is being learned and when it is later recalled. It also requires the activation of the hippocampus both for its encoding and retrieval (Siegel, 1999).

Memory and Self

Unlike semantic memory, episodic memory is the autobiographical recall of one's life experiences. It is linked to the tensing of time into past, present, and future, distinctions that entail the participation of the left frontal cortex. Episodic memory allows one to travel back in time to create a coherent narrative, and it is a requirement for the conscious construct of self, in which mind

Table 5.1   Types of Memory and Requirement for Hippocampal Activities

Type of Memory	Hippocampal Requirement
Explicit	
Semantic	Yes (Left)
Episodic	Yes (Right)
Implicit	
Procedural	No

reflects on its own experience. As the Buddha recognized 2,500 years ago, notions of causality and continuity create the false impression of a permanent self. However, today both Buddhist psychologists and most cognitive scientists would agree that our sense of self is in fact composed of innumerable reconstructed moments in time.

If this sounds far-fetched—as it certainly might to someone who is considering the idea for the first time—let us consider what happens in watching a movie. Movies are individual pictures strung together and projected rapidly on a screen. Our brain is unable to process the frames rapidly enough to see them individually, so it averages them over time, yielding a perceptual illusion of continuity. Personal experience is also a string of separate mind moments that are perceived as being in linear continuity. All this is not a philosophical aside concerning ontology; it is a critical feature of how the placebo response can be explained.

The capacity for episodic memory appears at about 24 months of age together with the emerging sense of a self (Bauer, 1996). Prior to this age, memories are uncoupled from narrative experience. Unlike semantic memory, which is dependent primarily on the activities of the left hippocampus located in proximity to the language centers of the brain, episodic memory appears to be primarily integrated with the right hippocampus and the right orbitofrontal cortex, brain regions that are topographically proximate to the limbic system (Nelson & Carver, 1998). As a result, episodic memory frequently includes not only the details of past experiences but also elements of its original emotional tone.

Implicit Memory and Somatic Activity

Implicit memory refers to the set of recalled experiences that operate outside of consciousness. It includes procedural memories, such as how to ride a bicycle, drive a car, or play a musical instrument. Implicit memory does not require the hippocampus for either for its encoding or retrieval, as the capacity to generate implicit memories is present at birth. Some procedural memories are encoded *in utero* by the activities of what might be termed priority brain structures, which include the thalamus, the somatosensory cortices, the orbitofrontal cortices, amygdala, and anterior cingulate gyrus. Implicit procedural memories are not actually a part of psychological experience, if we require that consciousness be an aspect of what is perceived. They do, however, contribute extensively to subliminal neuronal processing, the evaluation of experience, emotions, and somatic physiology.

They are in large measure responsible for how we behave without knowing it.

Implicit procedural memories form the basis of the earliest schemata of how infants experience their environment (Stern, 1985). These include how autonomic nervous system tone and the sensorimotor maps of the body are configured. They form the ground of being by contributing to a somatic core of self-constancy. The evolution of the nervous system has by design purposefully limited what must be consciously attended to. Fortunately, we are not aware of the innumerable sensations and motor activities that contribute to our background experience, as it would undoubtedly overwhelm consciousness.

Consciousness is only the tip of the iceberg of experience, as depth psychologists have long intuited. Much of who we are represents programs of preformulated nervous activity. As Freud suggested, we are not masters in our own house, a fact that we are invariably astonished to discover and reluctant to accept. As we shall see, the placebo response is one of these subliminal procedural processes, which may explain why it has been so difficult for some to embrace both its reality and its importance.

All Is Discomfort

With this brief overview of neuroscience as background, a model of the placebo response can now be developed. The first step is to ground the model in observation, which requires elucidating the phenomenology of the placebo response. Again, by definition, the placebo response develops in a therapeutic interpersonal dynamic in response to an offer to treat. But what motivates someone to seek therapeutic attention? The answer is invariably a desire to find relief from discomfort. For now, let *discomfort* be defined as the spectrum of perceived unpleasant physical sensations or mental states.

Sensations can be divided into two broad categories. Exteroceptive sensations arise from a source within the outer environment and are sensed by receptors that detect light, sound, taste, smell, and touch. Interoceptive sensations, on the other hand, arise from within the body, and, here, unpleasant cognitions and affects are included, in much the same way that Buddhist psychology includes mind as a sixth sense.

How does the body respond to uncomfortable sensations? The biological servomotor stratagem includes an afferent stimulus, a central comparison of the stimulus to a preestablished norm, and an efferent motoric response. Even a single-celled amoeba can effectively detect changes in its environment, compare them, and respond based on its evaluation. But a highly organized nervous system has the advantage of complex responses that cannot be achieved in a less developed species. Consider what transpires on encountering a hot stove (Figure 5.8). Immediately on touching the stove, receptors in the skin emit impulses that are rapidly transmitted via sensory nerve fibers to the spinal cord. From the spinal cord, secondary impulses are conveyed to neurons that innervate the muscles of the arm and hand, completing the circuit. Concomitantly, nerve impulses are conveyed up the spinal cord to the brain. The probable immediate response is an aversive movement of the finger away from the hot stove, completing the primitive spinal reflex arc.

But in a complex integrated nervous system, this does not exhaust the range of possible responses. For example, the impulse transmitted to the brain may evoke a top-down response that includes integrated impulses from multiple levels along the neuraxis. For example, if this is not the person's first experience with thermal pain, pain will be automatically compared to painful memories, and the reflex behavior may be modified. It some cases it may even be possible for the subject, following a long program of conditioning to graded painful stimuli, to willfully ignore the pain—a feat that can be useful for an Indian fakir intending to walk on fiery coals.

Discomfort is not simply due to pathways that register a stimulus as noxious but also reflects the complex history of the individual. This explains why the same stimulus may evoke minor discomfort in one subject, excruciating pain in another, and pleasure associated with the pain in yet another. Patrick Wall (2000), an anesthesiologist who has investigated pain, emphasizes this point: "Pain is an unpleasant sensory and emotional experience associated with actual or potential tissue damage or described in terms of that damage.... Pain is always subjective" (p. 29). Wall further advises that genetics, gender, group pressure, and cultural values all contribute to the perceptions of

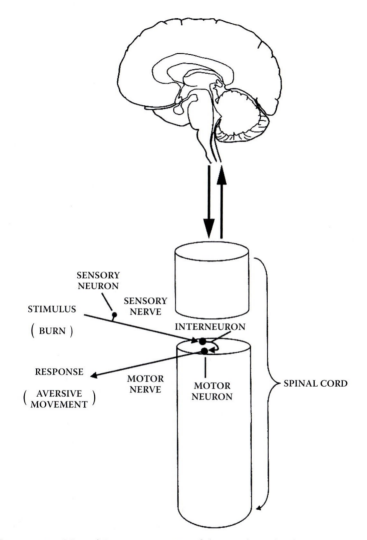

Figure 5.8 Neural Response to a Painful Stimulus. The diagram shows how a sensory stimulus is processed at the level of the spinal cord with information traveling up the neuraxis to the brain. The most likely response includes an aversive movement of the finger away from the stimulus, but, at times, these can be substantially modified by activities of the brain in a *top-down* response.

discomfort. In clinical practice, physicians frequently attest that women are less tolerant of pain than men. But this is not necessarily true. In one study, women showed a higher tolerance for heat-related pain than men, whereas men were better able to tolerate electrical shocks. This may reflect women's acquired experience with thermal burns in the kitchen and men's occupational conditioning to electrical shocks. Cultural differences in the ability to endure discomfort also form the basis of prejudices within society at large and the medical system in specific. Wall (2000) succinctly put it as follows:

> The whole world is populated by peoples assigned a place on a spectrum from extreme stoicism to utter impishness. Icelanders mock Danes, Swedes mock Norwegians, and I bet the Cook Islanders think the Sandwich Islanders a pretty cowardly group and vice versa (p. 67).

Most studies do not support such stereotypes. Despite this, prejudices can be so ingrained according to Wall (2000) that when a Canadian study failed to support the hypothesis that immigrant Chinese had a lower threshold to pain than native Canadians, the investigators concluded that the wrong groups had been selected rather than accept that there were actually no differences. Group pressure also contributes to the apparent increased ability of men to cope with pain. The initiation rituals among tribal peoples, the hazing experiences of college freshmen, and the rites of military boot camp all reinforce the value of enduring pain without complaint and explain why men may overall be less likely to seek medical attention than women. A patriarchal medical system can be inclined to devalue the willingness of women to seek care for what male doctors viewed as minor discomforts.

Physicians routinely assess whether reported discomfort is within the realm of likelihood. This exercise can have merit, but invariably it will go awry if the discomfort of another is criticized as exaggerated or false. As all discomfort is subjective; another simply cannot accurately evaluate it. Indeed, if there is any single attitude that impedes therapeutic benefit in practice, it is the failure to empathize sufficiently with the discomfort of another.

Thus far, it has been suggested that discomfort motivates patients to seek therapeutic attention, but discomfort is actually the perception of sensations that have been evaluated as negative. The valence of sensation is its *feeling tone*, and the attribution of feeling is a critical determinant of the placebo response.

Feelings Are Not Emotions

Discomfort is a negative feeling. Strictly speaking, feeling is not emotion; rather, it is the rational evaluation of sensory experience. But how and by whom is this evaluation made? For now, let us assume that there is an operational mind–body construct of self and that feelings are evaluated with respect to it. As we shall see, there can actually be more than one self-construct: one that is perceived and another that is not.

Recent research has contributed substantially to what is known concerning the neurophysiology of feeling. fMRI, a radiographic technique that allows investigators to visualize regions of the brain as they are activated in real time in response to stimuli, shows that the amygdala, a structure located deep within in the brain, plays a key role in the generation of feeling (Damasio, 1994). The amygdala is extensively connected to the sensory centers of the thalamus and to both cortical and subcortical regions (Figure 5.9). It is also well integrated with the hippocampus so that memories are able to influence the valence of feelings. The amygdala also contributes to the evaluation of threat and to fear and anxiety (McNally, Kaspi, & Riemann, 1990).

Feelings can be categorized as positive, negative, or neutral based on subjective reporting or by the observable behaviors that they evoke. However, discrepancies may exist between reported feelings, observed behaviors, neurophysiology. Acculturated individuals recognize that what one chooses to reveal to others may not necessarily reflect one's true feelings. Research has additionally demonstrated that feelings are registered subliminally and some never achieve consciousness (McNally et al., 1994). For example, sympathetic nervous system activation, the physiological response that characterizes fear, may be observed in subjects who deny feeling either fear or anxiety (Sifneos, 1996). Subjects may report feeling neutral about, for example, an angry face presented on a screen, whereas changes in heart rate and electrodynamic skin responses suggest that they are actually experiencing strong feelings.

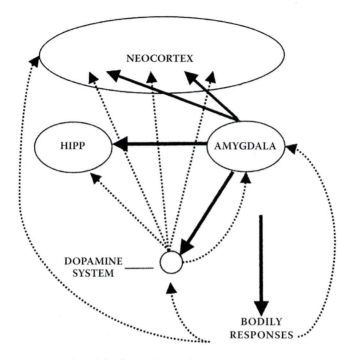

Figure 5.9 Feeling. The figure shows the connections among the amygdala, the dopamine system, the cortex, and the hippocampus (HIPP). The brain includes the method of evaluating the experience of the core self. This evaluation is called feeling. Whether experience is evaluated as positive or negative determines subsequent responses. At times, the reported feelings are discordant with what physiological measurements suggest, which may complicate some forms of placebo research.

Experimental evidence to support the role of implicit information processing in how feeling is generated has been derived from a psychological test referred to as the emotional Stroop paradigm (McNally et al., 1994). In this test, stimuli expected to evoke strong positive or negative feelings are presented as words represented by letters in different colors. The subject is asked to read a word and then rapidly to identify its color while pressing a button that times the response. Strong implicit feeling invariably increases the elapsed time from the stimulus to response—that is, the latency of response.

The test is a measure of what has been termed *filtering*. During the retrieval of the semantic memory (e.g., recollecting the word for *red*) required to respond accurately to the color of the presented word in the Stroop, the semantic associative networks of the mind must be scanned for the correct answer (Calvin, 2000). A highly valenced stimulus in the subliminal emotional Stroop paradigm produces feeling that cannot be filtered out and that consequently disrupts neural networks yielding a delayed response. If the subject was connected to sensitive instruments, one might also detect changes in heart rate, blood pressure, ventilation, and skin resistance as parallel evidence for sympathetic nervous system activation. The term *affect* is often equated with feeling, but its original definition was that of a feeling that could affect somatic activity, such as autonomic arousal. Psychologists today more often use it as a motivating factor in behavior. What is important to glean from this discussion is that feelings can affect both mental and physical activities concomitantly; they are both key elements in the functional mind–body connection.

The response to the Stroop might either reflect conscious supraliminal mental activities or implicit, subliminal activities. Can these be distinguished? In the *subliminal* emotional Stroop paradigm, a valenced word is presented on a computer screen for approximately 200 milliseconds, just long enough for the subject to visually register it, but too brief for it to be consciously perceived. Subsequently, a second neutral word is immediately projected on the screen that in effect masks the stimulus word. But the subliminal processing of the emotionally charged word is still able to delay the subject's response to the neutral word.

Preliminary experiments conducted in my laboratory have shown that when patients are challenged with lists of words that include medical references, such as *illness, disease, hospital,* or *doctor,* patients who exhibit high levels of conscious (supraliminal Stroop) or unconscious (subliminal Stroop) disturbances, subsequently are susceptible to developing placebo effects. This finding suggests that semantic associations to health-related terms may be emotionally charged for some patients and that subliminal negative feeling can be associated with placebo reactivity. Recall that Shapiro and Shapiro (1997) found that high levels of anxiety and depression, both of which are characterized by increased levels of negative feeling, were also predictors of placebo effects.

Why is this relevant to placebo research? One reason is that experimental approaches to placebo research are often based on patient self-reporting and that subliminal feeling is not considered. As conscious reporting may not reflect what is actually felt, this is a potential source of error. Feeling is also a portal into the mind–body conundrum and into recognizing how placebo effects are generated.

Well-Being: The Path to the Placebo Response

The result of the placebo response is the alleviation of discomfort and the restoration of well-being. Like discomfort, well-being is a complex perception, but unlike discomfort, it represents a positive evaluation of the state of the self. Whereas discomfort invariably triggers concern, well-being is generally taken for granted as the normal subliminal background state—that is, until it is lost. If we knew how background states of well-being develop, it might be possible to gain a deeper insight into how the placebo response recapitulates them.

A newborn infant appears to be experiencing discomfort much of the time. Babies are often fitfully crying or writhing in colicky discomfort. Certainly, that is how adult caregivers perceive the infant's experience, and in response, caretakers develop strategies aimed at alleviating the infant's distress. These may include feeding, holding, rocking, changing, warming, and singing to the child. Normally, these interventions are implemented serially and on an empirical trial-and-error basis until one is demonstrated to work.

The Reward System: Is the Placebo Response Related to Addiction?

But how might this subsequently create positive feelings in the infant? In the 1950s, researchers noted that rats responded to electrical stimulation of certain areas of the brain by returning over and over to the place in the cage where the stimulation had been administered. A site in the brain responsible for this behavior was localized to the site of a large bundle of axons called the median forebrain bundle (MFB), which tracks adjacent to the hypothalamus at the base of the brain. Further research demonstrated that the axons in the MFB projected primarily to neurons in the brainstem rich in the neurotransmitter dopamine (Bergman et al., 1989; Figure 5.10).

Animal models showed striking correspondence between brain-stimulation reward paradigms and the dopaminergic system (Bergman et al., 1989). Ablating dopaminergic areas in the brain, or pharmacologically blocking the effects of dopamine, succeeded in eliminating these pleasure-seeking responses. In addition, drugs with addictive potential, such as cocaine, were subsequently demonstrated to act by stimulating dopamine receptors. The involved brain regions, including the MFB, nucleus accumbens, and ventral tegmentum, were putatively termed the brain's reward system. In addition to dopamine, neurons in this pathway also produced serotonin, enkephalins, and opioid neurotransmitters that are recognized to contribute to the generation of positive feeling or hedonic tone. These are referred to as monoamine pathways.

Dopamine: A Key Regulator of Well-Being

A recent investigation has shown that dopamine is released primarily during the anticipatory phase of pleasure-seeking reinforcement (de la Fuente-Fernandez & Stoessl, 2002). But whatever

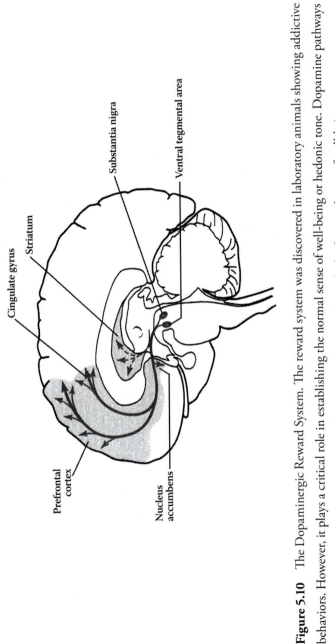

Figure 5.10　The Dopaminergic Reward System. The reward system was discovered in laboratory animals showing addictive behaviors. However, it plays a critical role in establishing the normal sense of well-being or hedonic tone. Dopamine pathways project from the brainstem to higher cortical centers and participate in the background state of well-being.

its specific role in hedonic responses, it undoubtedly plays an important role in the development of positive feeling. Dopamine is also a key neurotransmitter in the nigro-striatal pathways of the brain that participate in repetitive motor activities, so that rocking may promote positive feeling via activation of dopamine pathways.*

Parkinson's disease is an idiopathic—a fancy term for "no one knows the cause"—degenerative neurological disorder. Patients with Parkinson's develop characteristic pill-rolling tremors, gait disorders, and anhedonia, or decreased feelings of pleasure. The primary abnormality in this disorder is a deficiency in brain dopamine. De la Fuente-Fernandez et al. (2001) examined the PET scans of patients with Parkinson's disease who were told that they were to receive a drug that would help their Parkinson's disease but instead received a placebo.

PET detects radiolabeled substances and localizes them to specific areas in the brain. Patients who received the placebo underwent PET scanning of the brain following an injection of [11C] raclopride, a radioactive tracer that binds specifically to dopamine receptors. They found that patients who developed placebo responses exhibited reduced radioligand binding in the striatal regions of the brain, attributable to a local increase in endogenous dopamine release by neurons. This was the first

---

* Repetitive rocking movements are also a feature in the induction of mystical states, as evidenced, for example, by the role of movement in the Sufi whirling dervishes and Judaic *davening* during prayer.

study to demonstrate that a placebo intervention could lead to an identifiable and specific change in brain chemistry. It also raised the possibility that dopamine release might be responsible for the positive feelings of well-being that accompanied the placebo effect.

Placebo and Other Monoamine Pathways

Shortly after this study was published, Leuchter et al. (2002) at the University of Texas confirmed that a placebo was capable of yielding objective changes in brain activity. With PET, they showed that cerebral blood flow patterns, which reflect increased metabolic activities by activated neural circuits, were comparable in the placebo responders to those patients who had been treated for six weeks with the antidepressant fluoxetine (Prozac). Like Prozac, placebo yielded activation of the prefrontal cortex, premotor cortex, posterior insular, and posterior cingulate and decreased metabolism in the cingulate, hypothalamus, thalamus, insula, and parahippocampus. At roughly the same time, Mayberg et al. (2002) observed comparable changes in the PET scans of patients who had received the placebo instead of Prozac.

The specific neurophysiologic findings in these studies are complex and difficult to interpret. The major point, however, is that a placebo produced changes in the brain comparable to those caused by Prozac, a drug thought to reduce discomfort and to promote well-being by increasing brain serotonin levels. Psychopharmacologists include serotonin, along with dopamine and opioids, in the group of monoamine neurotransmitters that can specifically promote positive feelings. The findings from these studies are consistent with the hypothesis that the placebo response leads to positive feeling by increasing levels of brain monoamines. The next section examines how attachment theory and psychoanalytic inquiry can help to explain how mind and body may be integrated in the placebo response.

Learning Placebo: The Role of Functional Salutogenesis

Neurobiologist D. F. Smith (2002) proposed that the brain's repertoire includes activities that have evolved specifically for the purpose of promoting well-being. Smith termed this functional salutogenesis. As man is a social animal, many of these pathways include social interactions, including the placebo response. The brain regions Smith implicated in these responses—the pallidal striatothalamic regions, amygdala, and orbitofrontal regions—overlap with the findings of both Leuchter et al. (2002) and Mayberg et al. (2002), as well as with the reward pathways of the nervous system. Furthermore, they are comparable to those of the infant that mature in response to its interactions with caretakers and that are critical in regulating affect and autonomic system tone (Schore, 1999).

Whereas there are good reasons to posit that the capacity for mounting a placebo response is innate, it is not likely to be purely instinctual. Rather, it is more likely critically dependent—like most plastic activities of the nervous system—on interactions between nature and nurture that transpire in early life. In recent years, developmental psychologists have focused their attention on how these interactions determine how attachment develops and subsequently influences adult behavior.

Attachment

John Bowlby (1969), an English psychiatrist who pioneered attachment theory, took issue with Freud's theory of the primacy of the drives of sexuality and aggression and argued instead that the primary motivation of the infant was to attach to a stable caretaker. Attachment strategies are critical for mind–body development. The protoschemas of attachment serve as templates both for subsequent mental representations and somatic regulation. Indeed, the ideal place to start in developing a model of mind–body interaction is with the events of infancy, during which the mind is first integrated with somatic activities.

Pediatrician and psychoanalyst Donald Winnicott (1960) argued that there is no such thing as a baby; rather, there is only a maternal–infant unit out of which the child's autonomous behaviors differentiate. Attachment is largely evoked by discomfort, so it stands to reason that the early mental representations that develop during early attachment may also serve as templates for the placebo response. The parallels between attachment and the placebo response are so extensive as to suggest that they may be the same.

The newborn infant is ill prepared to fend for itself. It is neurologically immature; it cannot ambulate freely or feed independently. The period of human physical and mental development is the longest of all mammals, extending into teenage years and beyond that in complex modern societies. Attachment reduces the risks of starvation, exposure to the elements, physical attack, and separation from the group. In the absence of secure attachment—what Bowlby (1969) aptly referred to as a "secure base"—the life expectancy of the infant is significantly reduced.

Bowlby (1969) conjectured that a succession of increasingly sophisticated systems, including the brain structures that modulate arousal and emotion, are critically modified by attachment. From the perspective of developmental neuropsychology, the goal of attachment is to promote maturation of the brain regions responsible for configuring a progressive hierarchy of behavioral organization (Main, 1995). This is achieved by progressively bringing lower levels of primitive reactivity, such as the spinal reflexes, under the influence of higher cortical brain areas via top-down regulation (Toates, 1998). This organization of the early self is integrally linked to, and motivated by, the brain's affect centers. What psychologists term developmental stages are, in reality, new categories of dynamic skills that emerge with the progressive maturation of the nervous system.

Sensory Maturation

The basic substrate of psychological organization is sensation. As Freud (1923) noted in the "Ego and the Id," the first ego (I) is a body-ego, thereby emphasizing sensation as the primary mode of experience. The phylogenetically primitive olfactory-gustatory (smell-taste) system of the brain is the oldest organ of sensation. It allows the infant's capacity to make rudimentary discriminations with respect to its environment. For the most part, the olfactory centers of the human brain are proportionately smaller than those of other mammals, and man is ill prepared to evaluate his environment predominantly via his sense of smell.

Touch is required to develop a sensational map of the body surfaces.* This map allows the infant to recognize where the body container ends and the environment of nonself begins. Infants who were not adequately held may find it difficult as adults to establish optimal psychological and physical boundaries, as the former depends on the latter. These individuals may also report difficulties in the ability to self-soothe, a strategy that is closely related to the placebo response. The ability to evaluate sensation is necessary to respond appropriately to both the environment and the inner milieu.

---

* There is a meditative exercise in which the mediator is asked to scan the body map for evidence of sensation. It is a curious task, and most meditators will report idiosyncratic lacunes in their map.

At birth, the amygdala is sufficiently developed to evaluate sensation and to participate in the modulation of autonomic arousal. It also assists in the discrimination of olfactory sensation, so that the newborn infant can distinguish the maternal breast from that of a stranger by attraction or aversion, respectively The amygdala also modulates the activities of the hypothalamic nuclei that release vasopressin and oxytocin, hormones that can counteract stress-mediated autonomic arousal and can promote attachment immediately following birth (Schore, 2003). Cortisol released by hypothalamic activation of the anterior pituitary gland has widespread activities that include increasing blood sugar, decreasing inflammation, and either promoting or disrupting the registration and encoding of memory by hippocampal neurons.

At eight weeks of life, the infant's visual system becomes salient. With its maturation, the organizational control of the nervous system shifts from subcortical to cortical regulation, where it remains. Vision plays an enormous role in human activities. The synchronization of affect between mother and infant during attachment is coordinated primarily via gaze-related attunement. Limbic circuits specialized for assessing social intention show extensive reciprocal connections with the dopaminergic neurons that contribute to positive feeling. How we "see" the world metaphorically suggests how important vision is in the maturation of higher cortical processes.

Somatic Regulation

Perhaps the most critical early developmental task for the infant is to learn how to regulate its somatic activities. These include modification of sleep–wake cycles and the modulation of autonomic nervous system tone. These activities are strongly influenced by attachment. Psychologist Myron Hofer (1984) proposed that the early caregiver is a *hidden regulator* for somatic activities, providing physiological feedback that both entrains and modulates the infant's levels of autonomic nervous system arousal.

Parasympathetic nervous, or vagal, tone that evolves in an experience-dependent manner over the first two years of life counters the arousal mediated by the sympathetic nervous system. The result is a balance of these influences, one tending to promote chaos and the other order. There is also abundant evidence to suggest that the right hemisphere dominates the regulation of somatic activities. These activities are encoded via subliminal pathways that are not linked directly to consciousness or to language and ideation (Figure 5.11).

But how does the brain learn these responses? The most likely answer is via Darwinian competition between neural pathways. The repetitive activation of pathways that regulate autonomic tone, sensorimotor maps, and background emotional tone encodes information that is stored and recalled as implicit procedural memories of mind–body states. Some of these pathways are repetitively reinforced, so that their synaptic strengths

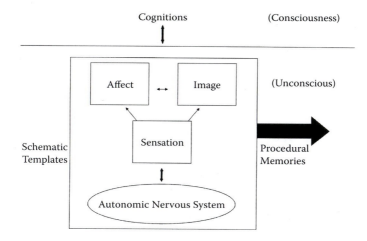

Figure 5.11　Mind/Body Schemata. The basic mind–body connections develop during infantile attachment to their caretakers. The earliest schemata include a somatosensory map that is linked to affect and image, and eventually to cognitions. These schemata contribute to the development of subliminal procedural memories that can be evoked later in life by the therapeutic interaction as the placebo response.

may be sufficiently high to ensure that they will be repetitively reselected from moment to moment as loop activities. This strategy yields repetitive momentariness and the illusion of cohesive somato-sensory-affective states of self.

Concomitant with these states, the mental representations of the social attachments in which they were learned are concomitantly encoded as elements of memory. As during the first two years of life, they are predominantly registered in the absence of left hippocampal and prefrontal cortical participation. As a result they are imaginally rather than linguistically mentally represented. Although they are not directly available for autobiographical narrative formation, they constitute an integral part of the regulation of somatic activities, so evoking these early imagistic schemas will concomitantly activate the procedural memories that mediate somatic activities. What is developing is a strategy via which early mental events are linked with regulation of somatic processes—that is, a prototypic strategy for evoking the placebo response.

The capacity to self-soothe is lost in the severe psychopathology known as borderline personality disorder. These patients report overwhelming anxieties due to a sense of disintegration of self. In most of these cases, the early childhood of these patients was distinguished by profound failures of attachment. The host of mental difficulties that characterize this disorder—including ambivalence, disordered affect regulation, interpersonal difficulties—may be accompanied by severe psychosomatic symptoms.

Placebo as Protosymbol

Neuropsychological maturation builds progressively in a bottom-up process on templates of mind–body activity. However, in time top-down processes also participate in modulating subliminal activities. But the question of how mind becomes a factor in interacting and influencing somatic function has not yet been answered. Mental activities develop on a scaffolding of sensations and affects. Somatosensory schemas are inextricably linked to affect; these in turn are integrated with images as the visual system matures. Finally, cortical centers of the left brain intervene. By that time, a complex associative map of somatic sensation, affect, and image, has already been established. Cognition is the final layer of regulation. From this perspective, the idea that mind and body are distinct is patently absurd, as cognition is only one aspect of an inextricably coordinated system of nervous activities.

Positive feeling is achieved via interpersonal sensory exchanges that establish the basic schemas. It is later modified by imagery and by cognition. The latter mitigates the perceptions of chaos by virtue of the modulatory effects of, for example, meaning and expectation. These form part of a complex associative map that is linked to positive feeling. As a result, well-being can be promoted by, for example, touch, gaze attunement, imagery, and meaning, with the likelihood that multiple modalities offer potent reinforcement.

With respect to mind–body interactions like the placebo response, the level of mental function is best termed protosymbolic. Winnicott (1959) suggested that the infant's capacity to self-soothe was promoted by transitional objects. When the infant's caregivers are not available, transitional objects such as a blanket or a teddy bear can serve as early surrogate sources of comfort. Psychologist Donald Bakal (1999) suggested that placebos act as transitional objects by evoking mental schemas of early dynamics with caretakers that can promote states of mind–body well-being. Bakal argued that separating at least some patients from their placebos can evoke the same discomfort that removing a blanket or teddy bear does for the infant.

These transitional objects, Winnicott (1959) argued, are mental amalgams of objective sensory reality combined with infantile fantasy. The merging of these elements to form a novel mental representation is what he termed a protosymbol. These serve several important functions in mind–body development. First, they are the templates for sophisticated symbol formation, e.g., in the form of metaphoric abstraction. They will contribute to how the infant, and eventually the adult, tends to construe meaning from its experience. An important function of the protosymbol is to link the subcortical and right-brain schema of somato-sensory-affect-image with the left brain's novel capacity for cognition. This allows cognition to participate as an emergent stratum of neurological organization in the service of self-soothing.

Positive Feeling in the Background

Psychoanalyst Joseph Sandler examined psychological motivations from the perspective of object-relations theory (e.g., Sandler & Sandler, 1998). In contrast to classical psychoanalytical drive theory, this school of psychoanalytic focuses on how mental representations develop and interact dynamically in the production of mental states and behaviors. Sandler speculated that positive feelings contribute to the emergence of a benign super-ego—that is, a symbolic mental representation of a benevolent caretaker whose primary role is to sustain a background experience of well-being. In other words, an internal and subliminal representation of a benevolent caretaker evokes background states of positive feeling, much as the physical presence of a benign caretaker in proximity to the infant can be enough to limit mind–body discomfort.

Sandler and Sandler (1998) recognized that background affects of well-being were critical to normal development and could be reestablished by fantasies and memories:

> Initially this (positive) affective state, which normally forms a background to everyday experience, must be the state of bodily well-being....
> This affective state later becomes localized in the self.... The maintenance of this central affective state is perhaps the most powerful motive for ego development (p. 11).

Disturbances in this background state motivate the distressed ego to seek external objects—either a person or a transitional object—that can reestablish these states. The conditions described by Sandler and Sandler (1998) closely parallel the conditions that evoke placebo effects. As Thomas (1987) demonstrated, even brief contact with a benevolent health care provider can promote placebo effects. This is achieved not by providing a specific treatment but by offering an opportunity for the patient to reexperience an implicitly remembered interaction with a soothing early caregiver. If it happens that an intervention is also offered, either as active drug or as placebo, it may be experienced as a transitional object that can evoke the background state of well-being.

It is evident that early developmental interactions include all of the elements that are recognized to contribute to the placebo response. But there is a great deal more to consider.

The Nocebo Response: Not All Placebo Effects Are Rewarding

The predilection for bivalent responses by the nervous system suggests that a negative placebo, or nocebo complex, must also exist. The nocebo response was encountered earlier during this volume's discussion of expectancy and meaning, but here it is examined in more depth and its relationship to the placebo response elucidated. Evans (2004) criticized the nocebo response literature for failing to rigorously prove that it actually exists. Certainly all of the arguments raised for placebo effects apply as well to nocebo effects. It will not profit us to shed further doubt on their metaphysics.

The nocebo response is well known to caregivers. Consider the following example from clinical practice. B is a 58-year-old man who suffers from inflammatory bowel disease with debilitating symptoms. He is anxious with a low threshold for discomfort. Whereas the pathology of his disease has been assessed as relatively mild, he reports a litany of abdominal and other somatic complaints. Unfortunately, any effort to medicate his discomfort exacerbates one or another of his symptoms. He is ostensibly eager to try new treatments but invariably cannot tolerate them. Suggestions that he seek some mode of supportive psychotherapy have consistently been rejected.

Approximately 25% of patients receiving a placebo report adverse side effects. In placebo trials for disorders that produce minimal symptoms (e.g., hypertension), nocebo effects are comparable to those seen with an active drug. The most common adverse symptoms include headache in 7%, somnolence in 5%, weakness in 4%, and 1% each in nausea and dizziness. In some studies, fatigue and gastrointestinal symptoms both occurred in approximately 15% of subjects. The severity of these symptoms may be sufficient to warrant withdrawing the subject from clinical trials. Few patients are aware that placebos can also produce side effects. As a result, one potential advantage of nocebo effects is that they may actually help to clarify the actual specific side effects caused by an active drug in a clinical trial.

The same mechanisms implicated in placebo effects including conditioning and expectancy are demonstrable in nocebo effects (Shapiro & Shapiro, 1997). Conditioned nausea occurs in one third of chemotherapy patients and may be triggered by incidental environmental cues, like the color of the treatment room. The mere suggestion that a drug can cause a specific side effect can seem like a self-fulfilling prophecy for some patients. The language adopted to describe the side effects of a drug can greatly influence expectancies and outcomes (Barsky et al., 2002). In one study, instructing subjects to look for evidence of nasal obstruction evoked more upper airway symptoms than instructing them to pay attention to the free passage of air. Drug inserts that describe a seemingly endless number of possible reported side effects have short-circuited the efficacy of countless numbers of prescriptions.

Nocebo effects represent a major problem for both medical management and health-care costs. Barsky et al. (2002) reviewed the role of the nocebo response in adverse responses to prescribed medications. This group noted that drug-related adverse events accounted for 76.6 billion dollars in hospital costs and for 17 million emergency visits in 1995. In one study, 11% of adverse effects were attributable to the medication, whereas the remainders were of questionable attribution. These authors specifically noted that statistics concerning penicillin allergy, which has a reported prevalence of 10% in hospitalized patients, actually support the conclusion that 97% of adults and 94% of children are able to tolerate oral penicillin and that the common side effects attributed to the antibiotic were either nonspecific or nocebo effects.

However, comparable with placebo effects there are many reasons for patients to misattribute adverse symptoms to medications. In addition to the nocebo response, these include confusion between the symptoms of the underlying disease and a drug side effect and the misattribution of endemic physiological dysfunction to medication. When Reidenberg and Lowenthal (1968) polled a healthy population that was not receiving medication, 39% described fatigue, 26% difficulty in concentrating,

23% drowsiness, 14% headache, and 5% dizziness. Only 19% reported having been asymptomatic over the prior three-day period. This finding was confirmed in a study that found that 73% of 236 healthy volunteers who were not taking medications reported adverse symptoms in the preceding three days (Barsky et al., 2002).

Nocebo effects have at times occurred under unusual therapeutic circumstances. Herbert Benson, a mind–body specialist at Harvard Medical School, recently assigned three Christian prayer groups to pray for patients who were undergoing coronary artery bypass graft surgery in six medical centers throughout the United States (Benson et al., 2006). These patients were not selected for their underlying religious beliefs or affiliations. The study found that 1,800 patients undergoing coronary artery bypass graft surgery did not do better when prayed for by strangers (i.e., through intercessory prayer) than those who received no prayers. This might have been the scientific expectation, but in fact these patients actually did worse. Of patients who were informed that they were being prayed for, 59% developed complications compared with 52% of those who had been told it was a possibility that they might be prayed for—a statistically significant difference. According to *New York Times* journalist Benedict Carey (2004), there is precedence for prayer evoking nocebo effects in other clinical trials:

> If researchers are struggling to prove that intercessory prayer has benefits for health, at least one study hints that it could be harmful. In a

1997 experiment involving 40 alcoholics in rehab, psychologists at the University of New Mexico found that although intercessory prayers did not have any effect on drinking patterns, the men and women in the study who knew they were being prayed for actually did worse. "It's not clear what that means," said Dr. William Miller, one of the study's authors.

Nocebo and Developmental Pathology

Anxiety, depression, and somatization all predispose to nocebo effects. Barsky (1992) demonstrated that heightened awareness of interoceptive cues including autonomic sensations is associated with nocebo responses. There is general agreement that secure attachment protects against psychopathology (Fonagy, 2001); in fact, as Michael Ainsworth, an expert on attachment noted, secure attachment may be "the primary defense against trauma-induced psychopathology" (Kumin, 1996). As previously noted, secure attachment develops through reciprocal mutually attuned preverbal interactions between mother and infant. When separated from the mother, the child engages in exploratory behavior, eventually shows signs of missing her, and subsequently returns to reestablish physical contact with her. Under good enough circumstances, the child develops the ability to self-soothe and a cohesive sense of self.

As opposed to optimal attachments, insecure-avoidant and chaotic attachments are associated with increased frequencies of psychiatric disturbances that include the inability to develop consistent relationships with others. Mothers of insecure-avoidant infants actively thwart physical proximity to their children, either by avoiding them or actively distancing them. Adult patients with avoidant and resistant attachments may show limited benefit from relational interventions (Fonagy, 2001). They may display little interest in others, tend to be cynical concerning their motivations, and are excessively self-reliant. Eagle (1999) suggested that avoidantly attached individuals are also prone to developing somatic symptoms and illnesses.

Insecure-ambivalent and chaotic attachments develop in settings where maternal caretaking has been inconsistent and confusing (Lyons-Ruth, 2001). These mothers alternate between efforts at inappropriately arousing the infant to meet their own needs and disregarding them. Unlike the avoidant infant, these children compulsively seek out attachment and may become anxiously distressed in its absence. They are often preoccupied with their internal distress and tend to seek help in self-soothing, often with little consistent success.

Psychopathology and Brain

As might be expected, difficulties with attachment negatively affect the hierarchical maturation of the developing nervous system. The evidence for anatomic and biochemical disruption of neural pathways in the developing brain due to suboptimal attachment is substantive and increasing. For example, studies suggest that deficits in attachment lead to changes in the postnatal development of biogenic amine systems, including the dopamine pathways. The cortical projections to dopaminergic neurons are particularly susceptible to disruption due to attachment-related traumas (Schore, 2003).

Severe, frequent, and intense disruptions in attachment lead to high levels of excitatory neurotransmitters, including glutamate, as well as to excessive activation of the hypothalamic-pituitary-adrenal (HPA) axis. High levels of glutamate are neurotoxic and yield neuronal loss and synaptic elimination, particularly in the hippocampus. This can potentially interfere with the development of somatosensory schemas. Damage to the amygdala in infancy can lead to profound deficits in the development of social bonding and in emotionality. Abnormalities in the development of the orbitofrontal region, which is highly susceptible to neonatal attachment trauma, can further distort the amygdala's response to highly valenced stimuli. Early relational trauma impairs the generation of a normal somatosensory map so that the experience of the body and self–other discrimination are disturbed (Craig, 2002).

Attachment trauma also yields persistent right-hemispheric dysfunction. The right brain hemisphere is densely connected to the emotional limbic regions and to autonomic and HPA pathways. It also plays a critical role in the encoding and retrieval of implicit procedural memory formation. Unmedicated children with attention deficit hyperactivity disorder (ADHD) show disruption of right hemispheric attentional systems (Carter et al., 1995). Furthermore, patients with developmental attachment trauma show an increased incidence of *alexithymia*, a profound defect in emotional recognition and the interpretation of interoceptive cues (Sifneos, 1996). This may manifest as an element in a variety of severe psychopathologies as well as in increased susceptibility for developing somatoform disorders (Rotenberg, 1995):

> Functional deficiency of the right hemisphere ... may be caused by the lack of emotional relationships.... If these relationships are insufficient, the right hemisphere will become insufficient, its contribution in psychological defense mechanisms and emotional stabilization will be lost, and there will be a general predisposition to subsequent mental and psychosomatic disorders (p. 59).

As Winnicott (1960) noted with characteristic poignancy, "If maternal care is not good enough, then the infant does not really come into existence, since there is no continuity in being; instead, the personality becomes built on the basis of reactions to environmental impingement" (p. 54). Another way of framing this statement is that the absence of good enough attachment leads to an abnormality in the structuring of core self-states. From the perspective of the placebo response, this might be expected to manifest as problems in generating stable background states of well-being. What ensues instead is a persistently dysphoric mood, or what psychiatrists term dysthymia, often accompanied by persistent somatic discomfort and affectual numbing. In other words, these patients show limited capacity to develop placebo responses. The background affect that is linked to their core self-construct is primarily negative, and, as result, they are prone to nocebo responses.

Until recently the link between disordered attachment and what may be nocebo effects in psychotherapy had not been considered (Kradin, 2004b). Freud (1914b) attributed therapeutic failures in his narcissistic patients to their limited capacities to develop transference. These patients, from the perspective of attachment theory, have had developmental histories of avoidant attachment, and their dominant early experience with caregivers was disappointment and discomfort. Freud was perhaps correct in concluding that these patients were unlikely to benefit from psychoanalysis, but the reason may be attributable to their inability to develop the salutary effects of the placebo response in the presence of their analyst caregivers.

Negative Therapeutic Reaction and the Nocebo Response

The entrenchment of a negative background feeling of self favors nocebo responses, and this may be expressed via negative therapeutic reactions in psychoanalytic treatment. According to Freud (1923), some patients not only do not positively benefit from the analytical experience of transference but actually do worse:

> Every partial solution that ought to result, and in other people does result, in an improvement or a temporary suspension of symptoms produces in them, for the time being, an exacerbation of their illness; they get worse during the treatment instead of getting better. They exhibit what is known as a "negative therapeutic reaction." There is no

doubt that there is something in these people that sets itself against their recovery and its approach is dreaded as though it were a danger (p. 49).

Consider the following example. K is a 32-year-old woman who carried the dual psychiatric diagnoses of borderline personality disorder and self-defeating personality disorder.* She was seen three times weekly in psychotherapy. Her childhood included paternal sexual abuse, parental alcoholism, and placement in numerous foster homes. Chaotic attachments and conflict persistently characterized her interpersonal relationships. She suffered from a variety of psychosomatic disorders that required frequent hospitalizations. Approximately five years into the treatment, she developed disabling chronic fatigue. Virtually all efforts to alleviate her physical and mental suffering either failed or yielded exacerbations of her symptoms. She was impossible to soothe.

Freud (1936) attributed this response to unconscious guilt in response to a harsh superego, as opposed to Sandler and Sandler's (1998) benign superego discussed earlier. According to Freud, "If you follow the analytic way of thinking, you will see in this behavior a manifestation of the unconscious sense of guilt, for which being ill, with its sufferings and impediments, is just what is wanted" (p. 137).

According to Melanie Klein (1986), an early psychoanalyst whose ideas diverged from Freud's in many areas, archaic

---

* This diagnostic criterion included in *DSM-IV* is an essential characterization of what might also be termed a "nocebo" personality disorder.

persecutory elements of an infantile superego contribute to the persistence of psychosomatic distress. In other words, the normal infantile distress in some infants has not been sufficiently transformed. Wilfred Bion (1962), a Kleinian oriented psychoanalyst, termed the early raw somatosensory experience of dysphoria elements and suggested that the primary role of the maternal caregiver was to assist the infant via a process he referred to as α-function in transforming these inexplicable negative sensations into mental representations and, subsequently, into language. To Bion, this dynamic was the basis of cognitive modulation of somatic sensation, providing a psychoanalytic link to Moerman's (2002) emphasis on meaning and placebo effects.

According to Bion (1963), when there has been serious maternal failure with respect to this task, the infant will suffer from a persistent inability to construct meaning out of interoceptive dysphoric sensations, and later will report persistent psychosomatic dysphoria. Adopting this as a metapsychological explanation, it can be hypothesized that nocebo effects are an expression of a patient's inability to benefit from caregivers, as they failed in their task of teaching the infant to self-soothe.

Michael Fordham (1978), a Jungian analyst, conceived of these counterdependent responses within psychoanalysis as part of the infant's defense of its psychophysical core experience and referred to them as defenses of the self:

> As the analysis progresses, especially in more difficult and more
> disturbed patients such as those with character disorders or borderline

cases, the resistance becomes more drastic … in some cases with severe failure in the development of self representation resistances seem to become so total that nothing the analyst says is acceptable—it is to be denied, attacked, misunderstood or confused…. (p. 74).

In many respects, the nocebo response is the mirror image of the placebo response. But unlike the placebo response that is organized as a subliminal effort to reestablish a background state of well-being, the nocebo response yields a background of negative feeling. For this reason, efforts to ally with the patient in the service of promoting well-being are invariably resisted and even countered in an effort to preserve the core background of dysphoria. In practice, caregivers have described these patients as help-rejecting complainers, and this is an accurate representation of who they are—although the pejorative implications are neither fair nor helpful as they have been behaviorally conditioned since infancy to preserve their configuration of self and background feeling tone. Their complaints are genuine; unfortunately, they cannot control a conditioned response that is beyond their awareness.

Placebo–nocebo responses can be said to depend on the maturation of specific brains structures and neurochemical pathways. But if this is the case, not only should psychopathology impede placebo responses, but also abnormalities in the underlying critical pathways should lead to placebo pathology. Is there evidence for such a claim? The answer is yes, and is discussed in the next section.

Placebo Pathology: Are Placebo
Responses Subject to Disease?

Few studies have critically addressed whether placebo effects are primarily affected by physical and mental disorders. Since all therapeutic effects potentially develop on bedrock of placebo effects, defects in placebo reactivity might be expected to decrease the magnitude of salutary responses—not only to placebos but to other therapeutic interventions as well. Those disorders classified as functional—that is, attributed to physiological dysregulation but with no apparent morphological basis—show the highest rates of placebo effects.

In a review of placebo response rates in clinical randomized trials of analgesics, Benson, Klemchuk, and Graham (1974) found that pain relief was reported by 30% of patients with migraine headaches. Freeman and Rickels (1999) examined the results of randomized clinical trials of premenstrual syndrome and found that that 20% of placebo responders reported sustained improvement and 42% exhibited partial improvement, defined as a decrease of 50% in a standardized premenstrual syndrome symptom score. Patients with functional dyspepsia showed an overall 20% placebo response rate that included 10% reporting the total eradication of symptoms (Lanza et al., 1994)—a response rate that is not substantially less than that observed with proton-pump inhibitors, the largest selling drugs on the market. The placebo response in patients with erectile dysfunction is also comparable to sildefanil (Viagra) and its recent congeners (Moore, Edwards, & McQuay, 2002).

Obsessive-Compulsive Disorder and Placebo

The highest placebo response rates are definitely seen in psychiatric disorders with some notable exceptions. Gavin Andrews (2001), an Australian psychiatrist, reviewed the placebo response rates in depression and in other psychiatric disorders in an article titled, "Placebo Response in Depression: Bane of Research, Boon to Therapy." Data from the Quality Assurance Project (1983), a meta-analysis of the major mental disorders in the mid-1980s, were reviewed. Placebos were found to account for 60% of therapeutic responses in major depression and 53% in general anxiety disorder, but only 23% in obsessive-compulsive disorder. In a separate study, a virtual absence of placebo effects was observed for patients with obsessive-compulsive disorder but not for patients with anxiety and panic disorders who showed high rates of placebo responses (Mavissakalian, Jones, & Olson, 1990), despite the fact that anxiety is thought to be a factor common to all of these disorders according to the current Axis I criteria outlined of the *DSM-IV* (2000).

In separate studies, treatment for compulsive shopping showed a high placebo response rate, whereas placebo responses for Tourette's syndrome and compulsive hair pulling, or trichotillomania, were low. Might certain forms of compulsive behavior include abnormal pathways that are not amenable to placebos?

Although the causes of obsessive-compulsive disorder have not been explicated, there is evidence that they may include abnormalities in the striatal pathways of reinforcement-reward system—that is, in the same or closely related pathways implicated in placebo responses. In addition, these patients often show muted or negative affect—so-called anhedonia—suggesting a defect in their ability to generate positive feeling.

ADHD and Placebo

ADHD shows lower placebo response rates than those seen in depression and anxiety. In one study, reported by Sangal and Sangal (2003) from the Attention Disorders Institute, less than 5% of subjects had a 60% or greater decrease in their ADHD-rating scales in response to placebo. Most forms of ADHD respond well to amphetamine and its congeners. Amphetamines act by blocking the reuptake of dopamine while releasing it from newly synthesized pools (Hyman, Malenka, & Nestler, 2006). They also inhibit the re-uptake of norepinephrine but exert little affect on serotonergic pathways. Both dopamine and norepinephrine are neuromodulators that have the capacity to increase the signal to noise ratio in neural networks, thereby enhancing the clarity of information processing (Spitzer, 1999).

When amphetamines are administered to normal subjects, they increase arousal and motor activity, but in children and adults with ADHD, they tend to normalize attention and diminish motor hyperactivity. Might the primary abnormality in

ADHD parallel a defect in the capacity for placebo responsiveness? Further studies are necessary to determine whether placebo responses to interventions other than those designed to target ADHD are also decreased in these patients.

Schizophrenia and Placebo

Although there are rare reports of excellent placebo responses in schizophrenia, the Quality Assurance Project (1983) found that placebo response rates in schizophrenia were also low. Schizophrenia is generally a progressive mental disorder characterized by severe symptoms including ambivalence, autism, and flat affect as well as by auditory and visual hallucinations. The disease has long been considered to have an organic basis and the concordance rate for monozygotic twins developing schizophrenia is 50% consistent with a underlying genetic predisposition to the disorder (*DSM-IV,* 2000).

In the 1950s, chlorpromazine (CPZ), a drug with antihistamine effects, was discovered to alleviate many of the symptoms of schizophrenia. Further research showed that CPZ blocked dopamine receptors, leading to the dopamine hypothesis of schizophrenia, in which it was proposed that excess dopaminergic activity was the cause of the disorder (Cohen & Servan-Schreiber, 1993). Although current evidence does not support this hypothesis, it does appear that dopamine plays an important role in this disorder.

One of the characteristic features of schizophrenia is the thought-disorder that these patients exhibit. As thoughts are difficult to monitor, disordered language communication has been adopted as a reliable surrogate marker for disordered thought (*DSM-IV,* 2000):

> The speech of individuals with schizophrenia may be disorganized in a variety of ways. The person may slip off the track from one topic to another; answers to questions may be obliquely related or completely unrelated, ... they may be so severely disorganized to be nearly incomprehensible (p. 300).

Cohen and Servan-Schreiber (1993), psychiatrists from the University of Pittsburgh, proposed that the thought disorder of schizophrenia reflects a decreased signal to noise ratio at synapses. Paradoxically, whereas drugs that inhibit dopaminergic activities are therapeutic in schizophrenia, they also appear to yield looser synaptic connections. The fact that both neural pathways formation and placebo response rates are disturbed in this disorder provides another piece of supportive evidence that the disruption of neural pathways may contribute to placebo pathology.

It is also noteworthy that schizophrenics suffer from an increased prevalence of somatic diseases. Many factors undoubtedly contribute to this, including high smoking rates and socioeconomic issues, but the failure to seek care-giving is notoriously common in this disorder and may explain why schizophrenia accounts for 20% of the homeless in this country, as many of these patients refuse to accept shelter even when offered (Folsom et al., 2005). Might this be a behavioral feature of a primarily disordered placebo response pathway?

Parkinson's' Disease and Placebo

Paradoxically, patients with Parkinson's disease have in several studies showed potent placebo responses. The characteristic feature of the neuropathology of Parkinson's disease is loss of pigmented cells in the substantia nigra of the pons and in other nuclei of the brainstem. Whereas there is an apparently normal age-related decrement in these pigmented neurons, patients with Parkinson's disease have fewer than 50% of what is expected for age (Shetty et al., 1999). These neurons produce dopamine, and tyrosine β-hydroxylase, the rate-limiting enzyme in the production of dopamine, is specifically decreased in Parkinson's disease. Currently, the treatment of Parkinson's disease focuses on the replacement of dopamine via administration of L-Dopa or one of its pharmacologic congeners. Recently, the surgical implantation of dopaminergic neurons into the brain has had some therapeutic success, and the possibility of curing this disorder via stem-cell replacement has been entertained.

Yet despite the loss of dopaminergic cells, placebo responses do occur in this disorder, and they have been associated with increased brain levels of dopamine. McRae et al. (2004) demonstrated that sham surgery for stem-cell replacement in Parkinson's disease yielded potent and long-lived placebo responses. Further implicating the importance of dopamine in placebo responses, Benedetti et al. (2003) recently demonstrated that the rate and pattern of neuronal activation in the subthalamic nuclei is modified by placebo in a manner that mimics dopaminergic stimulation. In a recent review, this group also outlined the neurobiological mechanisms of the placebo effect (Benedetti et al., 2005). Obviously, more research must be done prospectively to characterize placebo pathologies. But there is little reason to doubt that the observed differences in placebo rates in some disorders will prove to be caused by derangement in the physiology of this response.

The challenge remains as to how best to explain how placebo responses develop. Medicine makes no claim to overarching theories like a general theory of relativity in physics. Since the time of Hippocrates, Western medicine has preferred to eschew theory and to embrace empiric observation. However, in the absence of a guiding theory it is simply impossible to frame knowledge and scientific investigations. All of our knowledge is ultimately grounded in theoretical frameworks, so it is important to know which theory is being adopted.

6 The Anomalous Placebo Response

> The truth is that a great intellectual challenge must lie in understanding the overall logic of higher order systems.
>
> **D. Nobel and C.A.R. Boyd**

Introduction

A very basic question concerning the placebo response has been ignored. Indeed, nowhere in my research of this topic have I found reference to it, yet it is a glaring issue. It is simply the following: Are placebo effects the result of a unitary mind–body response or of many distinct responses? Placebo effects have been reported in virtually all areas of medicine, ranging from placebo analgesia to the reduction in tumor size, but what, if anything, might these have in common with respect to how they are mediated? Surely if each placebo response is different, then the idea of a monolithic placebo response must be in error.

This chapter begins by stating that it is impossible to explain a unitary placebo response via the dominant methods applied to medical science. Medicine is rooted in Newtonian physics, which includes two major principles that have already been encountered. The first is linear causality, which means that events follow in space and time in a direct and mathematically predictable manner and in response to forces acting on them. The other is reductionism, which posits that the material world can be analyzed by examining progressively smaller units of matter.

Let us begin by examining the latter. In the biomedical sciences, the penchant for reductionism has inspired scientists to reduce the body into progressively smaller units. The focus of medicine has progressively shifted from the study of the gross anatomy and physiology of the body as a whole to the microscopic observation of cells to the current emphases on molecular and genetic interactions.

As reductionists, many biomedical scientists believe that the causes of disease ultimately will be discovered via a detailed analysis of genetic and molecular elements. Indeed, the analytical approach has been eminently successful and continues to inspire instrumental progress. Unfortunately, it is also limited, as the following example demonstrates.

Suppose that you want to know what a thought is. This is a reasonable question that has been repeatedly asked but that nobody has yet been able to answer satisfactorily. How does the reductionist approach the question? Having first determined that thought is dependent on the human brain, scientists would begin by examining the brain for areas where thoughts appear to arise. We have a pretty good idea that the left prefrontal cortex is important, but we still do not know what a thought is. Next, they might examine that area of the brain under the microscope for its neuronal arrangements. Determining the roles of neurotransmitters and receptors might be important. Eventually, they might examine the atomic interactions between molecules at synapses. But after all of this has been done, scientists will not be any closer to the goal. Something about the approach is wrong-headed.

Scientific reductionism fails to answer the question because a thought is the product of a complex interconnected system of neurons called the brain. Such systems do not behave in linear ways; they are subject to different rules of behavior and require distinct methods of analysis. They can yield properties that cannot be predicted a priori from the underlying elements that contribute to their composition, a property termed emergence. Knowing everything that can possibly be known about the elements that produce a thought will not reveal what a thought is, because it is a fundamentally different phenomenon than the elements that produce it. René Descartes was correct: Mind and brain are categorically different, even if they are inextricably linked.*

---

* Many other examples could have been chosen. In fact, thought is a particularly poignant example because it suffers from also lacking materiality, making it an even more difficult nut to crack. Here the author is reminded of Johann Wolfgang von Goethe's text on optics in which the 18th-century literary genius writes in polemic form concerning the limitations of Newtonian science and its inability to describe the simplest of subjective experiences. To Goethe, knowing everything about how light behaves says absolutely nothing about the experience of vision.

Physicists since the beginning of the 20th century have accepted that quantum mechanics with its probabilistic implications is a better model of how atoms and energy interact than deterministic classical mechanics. When objects are moving at speeds approaching the speed of light, they adopt Albert Einstein's equations of special relativity as a more accurate description of the behavior of matter and space-time than Galileo Galilei's notions on these topics. Theoreticians and experimental investigators in the physical sciences have grown accustomed to, if not always entirely comfortable with, scientific pluralism. Yet medical scientists continue to champion Newtonian science to the exclusion of other approaches. But the biomedical sciences have lagged significantly behind the physical sciences in this realization. Philosopher Mary Midgely (2004) summarized the problem with respect to mind–body science in her monograph *The Myths We Live By*:

> The crude dualism that treats mind and body as separate, discon-
> nected things, still leads people to take sides between them and to sup-
> pose that having opted for the body, they must simplify the scene by
> ignoring the mind. The trouble lies in the exclusiveness, the either/or
> approach, the conviction that only one very simple way of thought is
> rational. Even within science itself, this simplistic approach is begin-
> ning to make trouble. Our familiar stereotype of scientific rationality
> is still one modeled on the methods of seventeenth century physics....
> For many purposes modern physics has moved away from those meth-
> ods. But not everybody in biology has heard the news of this change.
> Many biologists still tend to see mechanism as the only truly scientific
> thought-pattern because they still think that it is central to physics.
> And for some this belief has concentrated their attention strongly on

microbiological questions leading them to neglect large-scale matters such as the behavior of whole organisms (p. 21).

To illustrate what is being referred to, let us revisit the description of the response to touching a hot stove. Previously, this was described as a simple linear and causal response in which pain fibers in the skin carried an impulse to the spinal cord and then back to the muscles of the hand as well as to the brain. But there is in reality substantial complexity and interconnectedness in even this simple neural response. In fact, the impulse at the surface of the skin—let us call it nodal point a—is affected by all of its connecting pathways—that is, by nodal points b, c, d, e, and so forth. The neural impulses in the cortex are not only influenced by what is occurring at the skin surface, but they also modify what is occurring there. Indeed, it is impossible to describe with accuracy what is actually transpiring at any moment or place in such a complex system, because the possibilities are simply enormous. Luckily, however, although the levels of interaction are substantial, they are neither limitless nor unbounded.

It can be appropriate to apply linear approaches to complex phenomena when they yield answers that are ultimately accurate. There is no need to apply quantum mechanics or relativity even to events like landing a space ship on the moon, because empirically Newtonian mechanics does the job quite nicely. However, when Newtonian science fails to yield a good enough answer, then it should be abandoned rather than pursued further in attempting to force a square peg into a round hole.

Why is it difficult to transcend Newtonian approaches? The answers are complicated, but I think that we have already seen one in Hume's (1888) critique of causality. The mind naturally thinks in linear and causal terms. It is part of how the mind–brain is configured. To transcend this perspective, as Einstein and Niels Bohr, the champion of quantum theory, did, one must also be able to transcend one's experience. It is what might be termed an *opus contra naturam*—that is, a work against nature.

Fortunately, there are some preliminary signs that the dogmatic adherence to Newtonian ways of framing questions in medicine and biology is beginning to yield. At a conference I recently attended, a young cancer biologist was asked a question concerning the pathogenesis of cancer, obviously an area of some complexity. The question as phrased demanded the usual overly simplistic yes-or-no-type answer. To his credit, the young scientist politely demurred and instead indicated that we are only beginning to recognize the complexity of what cancer represents.

The Nonlinear Brain

If linear determinism and causality are inadequate to address complexity, is there currently a mode of science up to the task? Until recently in the history of science, the activities of complex systems were viewed as unpredictable and randomly chaotic.

Scientists attributed the erratic behaviors of a dripping faucet or the static of a television set to noise in the system, which is to say that they were not candidates for scientific explanation, because they were unpredictably random events. But by the end of the 20th century, scientists and mathematicians noted that some forms of chaotic activity were not random but actually deterministic (Gleich, 1988).

However, unlike Newtonian systems, the phenomena of deterministic chaos were nonlinear. A cardinal tenet of nonlinear systems is that their behaviors cannot be predicted with accuracy. In Newtonian mechanics by knowing the location of a particle in space, its momentum, and the forces that act on it, it is theoretically possible to predict its future behavior. But unlike Newtonian mechanics—and more akin to quantum mechanics, which accurately describes the physical world at the atomic or quantum scale—complex systems are probabilistic, which means that one can describe them only in terms of their most likely behaviors.

Another characteristic feature of deterministic chaos is exquisite dependence on initial conditions. This means that small changes in the initial conditions of two otherwise identical systems will lead to large difference in their responses. The example often given is how the infinitesimal changes in air movement caused by the beating of a butterfly's wings in Africa can lead to major changes in the weather in North America. The behavior of a nonlinear system is predictable in the short term, but it rapidly becomes erratic so that accurate projections concerning its long-term behavior are simply not possible. This is why the weather reporter is good at forecasting whether it will rain tomorrow but rarely gets it right in long-range predictions. In addition, the reader may recall that the difference between the human and murine genome is only approximately 1%. Yet even this small dissimilarity can lead to large differences in function when the system is complex, as life is.

Cognitive scientists soon recognized that the brain with its complexity and high level of connectivity met criteria for a chaotic system (Carver & Scheir, 1998). William Calvin (2000), a neuroscientist, suggested that differences in initial conditions might also influence neural activity and human behavior.

> There isn't a one to one (linear) mapping between spatial-only and spatiotemporal patterns within the nervous system in the manner of a phonograph recording or sheet music. A given long-term connectivity surely supports many distinct spatiotemporal patterns. ... It is presumably the initial conditions that determine which pattern is elicited from the connectivity (p. 65).

In other words, the properties of the nervous system at a given point in time—that is, its state—become the initial conditions for its subsequent activities. This implies that even minor changes in informational input from the outer or inner milieu can greatly alter the long-range behavior of the nervous system, a fact that has been appreciated by most observers of human nature. Yet a deeply ingrained sense of determinism continues to impel medical scientists to seek simple answers to complex questions, including the placebo response.

Are Attractors the Key to How Experiences Are Organized?

Nonlinear systems are neither beyond description nor completely unpredictable. When one mathematically models deterministic chaos, definite boundary conditions emerge. These can be detected by graphing the mathematical equations of deterministic chaos as a phase diagram (Carver & Scheir, 1998). The resultant curve represents the trajectory potential of the system over time. At any given point in time, the system must be somewhere within its trajectory, although it is not entirely certain where. However, the system is statistically most likely located in certain regions, which are called attractors (Figure 6.1). In addition, the system appears to actively avoid other areas termed repellers.

If one graphs the phase space of a system as a linear plot of its potential energies (Figure 6.2), the presence of peaks and troughs deviating from a baseline is appreciated. The troughs are areas of the system's lowest potential energies, which is the definition of an attractor. When the system is within a trough, it is stable and disposed to remain there. Repellers are represented by potential energy peaks, in which the system is energetically unstable and which it tends to avoid in its effort to return to a trough of attraction. As John Anderson, a computer scientist, observed with respect to the possibility that stable mental states

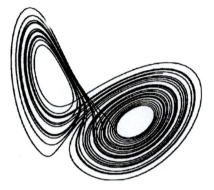

Figure 6.1 Phase Diagram of a Chaotic Response. The figure shows the graphic depiction of a so-called Lorenz attractor, which is a plot of a non-linear deterministic system. Such images may explain how the nervous system is capable of generating its own image of an attractor of its own core activities.

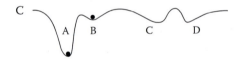

Figure 6.2 Linear Plot of the Potential Energies of a Chaotic System. Troughs represent the most potential energy minima of the system (black ball) and its most stable positions, termed attractors. Memory meets the definition of an attractor. Once a system's attractor is known, the system can be reconfigured even in the loss of some of its elements.

were neural attractors of the central nervous system: "The idea has an agreeable feel. Certainly, subjectively, we believe that meaningful mental states somehow are solid, coherent, and long lasting" (Anderson & Rosenfeld, 1988 p. 402).

The pattern of a deterministically chaotic system can be recreated by knowing its attractor, even when some of its elements
have been lost. This is precisely the kind of property that has
been attributed to memory, in which even small bits of information may be sufficient to succeed in reconstructing a complex memory. According to cognitive scientist Manfred Spitzer
(1999), "Even if the input is only similar to a stored input, the
activation pattern will converge on the closest attractor. In other
words, the network will spontaneously 'judge' similarity and
thereby generalize across a pattern of input patterns" (p. 171).

When we scan our minds to recall a name or a place, we
are looking for cues to assist the brain in its selection of the corresponding stable neural configuration. If we are successful,
the attractor, or memory, is selected and retrieved. This might
explain how the therapeutic dynamic evokes remembered states
of well-being in the placebo response.

Catastrophic Responses and the Restructuring of Experience

If our minds were nothing more than stored configurations of
attractors or memories, the result would be a hopelessly limited
rigid repertoire. How might a nonlinear system express its flex-
ibility? Catastrophe theory describes how systems can shift from
one attractor to another. It is a theory that includes discontinui-
ties, splitting, and bifurcations in its descriptions of the behaviors
of systems. It shares several features with chaos theory, including

emphases on nonlinearity and sensitivity to initial conditions. According to Charles Brown (1995), a catastrophe in phase space represents "The sudden disappearance of one attractor and its basin and the dominant emergence of another attractor" (p. 202).

But nonlinear systems do not merge imperceptibly from one attractor into another. Instead, they shift as discrete all-or-none transformations, like quantum electron jumps. Carver and Scheier (1998), psychologists who study the role of nonlinear dynamics in human psychology, referred to perceptual catastrophes, in which ambiguous images appear differently based on shifts in the perspective of an observer. In Figure 6.3, the perceptual shift from the image of the young woman to the old crone is complete, and no intermediate image combines both configurations. This is an essential feature of a catastrophic shift. Might catastrophe theory and deterministic chaos help in describing how placebo effects might be generated? Let us continue and see if this is the case.

The Placebo Response Complex

The shoe that fits one person pinches another; there is no recipe for living that suits all cases. Each of us carries his own life form—an indeterminable form, which cannot be superseded by another.

Carl Jung

If the placebo response is a result of nonlinear deterministic chaos, it should be subject to minor changes in initial conditions

Figure 6.3 Catastrophic Shift. The figure is an example of a perceptual catastrophic shift. One either sees the young woman or the old crone. The shift is complete and includes no intermediate image.

and consequently should exhibit limited predictability—which is exactly what is observed from empiric observation. But this still does not explain how placebo effects are generated or whether they are the result of one or many responses.

Let us now attempt to address these questions. To begin, I am going to postulate that the placebo response actually yields two potentially separable types of placebo effects. The first may be termed a shared, or public, effect, as it is common to all placebo responses. And what is common to all placebo responses?

The answer has already been discussed: All patients who develop placebo responses report restoration of their background state of well-being at least transiently.

The second set of placebo effects is ideographic or private. These effects counter the nonaffective symptoms (i.e., subjective) and signs (i.e., objective) associated with discomfort. Private effects can range from improvements in minor functional discomforts, such as headache or gastrointestinal upset, to objective effects, such as reduction in blood pressure or tumor burden. The total placebo effect can be represented *as a combination of its public and private effects* (Figure 6.4).

Private Effects

Previous chapters have examined how the background state of well-being learned in relationship to early caregivers is implicitly recalled by the placebo response. But an explanation has not yet been offered as to how one might account for the diversity of private placebo effects. One could conclude, as Hrobjartsson

Figure 6.4 Bipartite Placebo Effects. The total placebo effect is imagined to include a public or common effect of well-being and an idiosyncratic or private effect that mediates a return to normal physiology of the self.

and Goetzsche (2001) essentially did, in claiming that placebo effects were seen only with respect to subjective parameters—that the placebo response is actually limited to its public effect. But then we would have to ignore the countless reports of objective changes developing in response to placebos.

From the perspective of scientific economy, the idea of a multiplicity of unrelated private placebo effects lacks appeal. Adopting Occum's razor, it would be more efficient to explain placebo effects by a single stratagem. The question is whether there is evidence for such a stratagem.

Carl Jung and the Complex

Swiss psychiatrist Carl Gustav Jung was an eccentric genius (Figure 6.5). Today, most conventional scientists—but by no means all—tend to reject Jung's ideas as metaphysical or mystical. But his early career had serious scientific underpinnings. While working as a research psychiatrist with Eugen Bleuler, who coined the term schizophrenia, at the Burgholzli Hospital in Zurich in the early 1900s Jung noted that when patients were asked to give their immediate verbal associations to a set of stimulus words, certain words yielded delayed responses. He was not the first to examine this word association experiment (Aschaffenburg, 1904), but his research caught Sigmund Freud's attention and was soon widely recognized.

These indicator words also yielded evidence of autonomic arousal—increased heart rate, respiratory rate, and changes in

Figure 6.5   Carl G. Jung. A Swiss psychiatrist, Jung's early research with the word association experiment led to his concept of a complex, which represents the interconnectedness of somatosensory, imaginal, and conscious contents. The placebo response may be an example of what Jung conceived as the supraordinate homeostasis of self.

galvanic skin responses—all indicating activation of the sympathetic nervous system. Jung concluded that this response was caused by the detection of a complex (Jung, 1981). If the details of the word association experiment sound familiar to the reader, they should, as they are comparable to the emotional Stroop paradigm previously examined in our discussion of feeling.

Freud adopted the complex as the explanation for the disturbances that he had previously termed parapraxes (e.g., slips of the tongue) and attributed to an unconscious neurosis. People today think of a neurosis as a mental disorder, but that is not how Freud, Jung, and other early psychoanalysts originally understood them. A neurosis was a motif of mind–body dysfunction and was the cause of psychosomatic symptoms. The complex provided Freud with what he was originally seeking, which was a way of explaining how the mind might influence the activities of the body.*

From a modern perspective, Jung's complex can be conceived as a map of mental associations that is inextricably linked to a feeling tone as well as to a somatic state. It shares comparable features with mind–body schemata that develop during attachment in the infant. Jung also observed that a fundamental feature of the complex was its automaticity. Complexes spontaneously produced changes in mind–body states without dependence on conscious volition. He referred to complexes in his later writings as splinter personalities and suggested that at times they were so large and sufficiently charged with feeling as to interrupt normal waking consciousness with uncharacteristic thoughts, feelings, and behaviors (Jacobi, 1959).

In the extreme, this describes what is observed in multiple personality disorder—now termed dissociative identity diffusion disorder in the *DSM-IV*—in which extensive complexes dissociate from consciousness and emerge as distinct personalities, or alter egos. At times, complexes have been associated with profound changes in somatic physiology. In one documented case,

---

* For reasons that are not abundantly clear, the psychophysical importance of the complex was gradually lost. Today most refer to it with respect to, for example, the Oedipal complex or an inferiority complex. But this was not what Jung originally had described.

the alter ego of an otherwise physiologically euglycemic (normal blood sugar) patient with multiple personalities was demonstrated to be an insulin-dependent diabetic (Rossi, 1992).

Jung's idea of the complex captures many of the elements seen in placebo responses (Kradin, 2004). Although he never referred to the placebo response, Jung (1967) did suggest that complexes were the likely cause of psychosomatic disorders. He also suggested that the complex was mediated via an internal image. He described this as follows:

> What then, scientifically speaking, is a "feeling toned complex?" It
> is the image of a certain psychic situation that is strongly accentu-
> ated emotionally.... This image has a powerful inner coherence,
> it has its own wholeness and in addition, a relative high degree of
> autonomy so that it is subject to the conscious mind to only a limited
> extent.... (p. 98).

Might mental images mediate placebo responses? The idea at first sounds odd, but the fact is that images are linked to most responses by the nervous system.

How Is Self Dependent on Image?

In his recent text *Second Nature*, Edelman (2006, p. 92, italics in original) suggested the following way in which an image might precede behavior:

> An animal that evolved with a degenerate re-entrant set of circuits
> linking many cortical regions together could make enormous num-
> bers of discriminations and distinctions.... The pattern of integrative
> activity in this thalamocortical reentrant neural network, called the

dynamic core, would create a scene in the remembered present of primary consciousness, a *scene* with which the animal could lay plans.

Is there a mechanism via which an image might actually motivate an implicit response like the placebo response? In his text, Edelman (2006) proposes that there are two parallel dynamic cores: one linked to the language areas of the left brain, which mediates waking consciousness; and the other linked to the limbic-based structures of the right brain, which mediates changes with respect to somatic activities that are outside of consciousness. Empirical evidence for this is derived from a series of experiments conducted by Nobel laureate and neuropsychologist Roger Sperry in patients who had lost the anatomic neuronal connections between the right and left cerebral hemispheres (Erdman & Stover, 2000). These patients were able to perform a variety of complex tasks and to make decisions while showing functional independence of the right and left brains. But for the purposes of the present argument, what is important is that both systems of mental activity are potentially rooted in images—or what Edelman referred to as scenes in the remembered present.

Edelman and Tononi (2000) suggested that the uniqueness of the secondary neural repertoire may be imagined as a neurosignature of self, which not only mediates conscious experience but also regulates, for example, metabolic states, autonomic tone, and musculoskeletal posture. Large elements of somatic experience result from the repeated implicit activation of somatosensory maps encoded during development. The perceived solidity of self results from these implicit procedural memories, as they are repetitively selected by virtue of their synaptic strength.

These pathways are linked to a modular neural domain that includes the parallel activities of the amygdala and the dopamine reward-reinforcement pathways, in which the role is to monitor the activities of the somatosensory core and to establish and maintain its background feeling tone. Edelman (2006) said the following:

> The combination of value system activity, along with the selectional synaptic changes in specific networks of neuronal groups, governs behavior. Selection within these networks determines the categories of an individual's behavior; value systems provide the biases and rewards (p. 31).

This modular model of self parallels the proposed modular model of the placebo response (Figure 6.6), as it includes parallel contributions: one based on the establishment of feeling tone (i.e.,

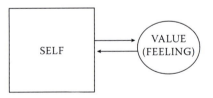

Figure 6.6 The Core Self with Modular Domains. The diagram shows the highly connected neural networks of the core self with input and output related to its valuation domain and to motoric effects on the body.

the public effect); and the other based on the selection of diverse somatosensory schemas (i.e., the private effects).

But how can an image emerge from these activities? Imagine that neurons of the dynamic core were somehow illuminated so that they could be visualized when activated. The illuminated activated dynamic core would yield an image corresponding to the system's most probabilistic configuration. Assuming that the core is the most stable energetic configuration of the neural system it would correspond to a supraordinate attractor, which, subjectively speaking, would also be the self. An observer located outside of the system could analyze this image, but it would also present an internal image. The constituent neural elements of the core could also be recreated based on the established attractor or image.

Attractors, Catastrophes, and Placebo

The model that is developing for the placebo response is based on the idea of self-regulation. Traditional medicine includes modes of regulation, but they are limited to the subsystems of the body. Models of homeostasis—*homeo* means same, *stasis* means position—have been applied to a variety of the body's activities. A simple homeostatic motif includes the up or down regulation of a cell membrane receptor in response to the local availability of its ligand. For example, receptors on fat cells bind to circulating insulin and increase in number when circulating insulin levels are low, but they will be reduced when excess insulin is locally available.*

When one develops a fever in response to an infection, cytokines—including IL-1, IL-6, and TNF-α, the so-called endogenous pyrogens—are released; we already encountered these molecules in the discussion of sickness behavior. These cytokines act by increasing a set point for body temperature that is set in the hypothalamus to correspond to a core body temperature of roughly 98.6°F to a new and higher level, such as 101°F. If the body temperature rises above this set point, the body responds by sweating to lower the core temperature. If it falls below the set point, muscles contract to produce shivering that raises the temperature back toward the set point. When the infection resolves, the set point reverts to its previously normal position.

This type of regulation is based on the nonlinear dynamic concept of a point attractor; this is an attractor with a so-called fixed basin of attraction or set point. This mode of homeostasis applies to a host of physiological activities, including blood pressure and electrolyte balance. However, serious consideration has rarely been given to extending the idea to include the supraordinate regulation of the human mind–body.† This may reflect the bias of allopathic medicine against the holistic approaches

---

* Type II, or adult onset, diabetes in many cases shows an abnormality in the homeostatic response of insulin receptors on fat cells.

† Except for Jung, who argued in a crude but characteristically prescient manner that the self was a homeostatic system.

that champion such ideas with little scientific explanation. But when reductionism is the guiding principle, it is easy to see why proposing a larger overarching principle of regulation would not be a priority. Yet the idea of a self-regulating self is attractive, as it might explain why the self naturally resists destabilization and has the ability like a gyroscope to spontaneously right itself.

How might such a system behave? Consider the following analogy. Let us say that an attractor governs a smoothly flowing river. When a modest amount of energy is introduced by the presence of the local resistance of a sandbar, the attractor resists the change. But if a high level of turbulence is introduced, as might be the case if the river approaches a waterfall, then the changes will exceed the ability of the attractor to absorb the new level of energy, and its behavior would either shift catastrophically to a new attractor or become truly chaotic. Are such catastrophic attractor shifts (Figure 6.7) germane to health and disease? Ary Goldberger, a Harvard scientist who has pioneered the study of nonlinear science in medicine, suggested as much, in his

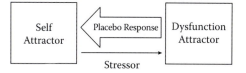

Figure 6.7 Placebo Response. The diagram shows the placebo response as an automatic catastrophic shift from an attractor of mind–body dysfunction back to its normal self-attractor.

analyses of what occurs, for example, in going from a normal heart rhythm to one that is pathological (Goldberger & West, 1987). Many examples of nonlinear determinism and attractor theory have been demonstrated to be relevant to human physiology and disease.

So at this point, a new definition of the placebo response can be offered:

> The placebo response represents a catastrophic shift that automatically moves the neural construct of self away from an attractor governing mind–body dysfunction and back to its previously established attractor of normality.

Why is this proposed definition attractive? For one, it explains how the large number of distinct activities required to mediate private placebo effects could be regulated by a unitary response. Certainly, a number of cellular and humoral events must contribute to the placebo response, and a traditional reductionistic approach would appropriately be aimed at detailing them. But that approach cannot discern or explain the overarching regulation of the system.

There is precedence for such a model in biology. Slime molds are colonies of unicellular organisms. Under appropriate conditions, the cells that comprise the slime mold function independently. But under stressful environmental conditions, such as a lack of nutrients, a sudden catastrophic shift occurs with all of the independent organisms self-organizing into a single supraordinate organism. Another example of a complex system, the human immune system, may help to reinforce the argument.

In the last 50 years, substantial progress has been made in understanding the mechanisms of how tissue grafts are rejected. Currently, many modes of treatment are based on organ transplantation. But for the transplant to survive, the immune response must fail to reject it. The problem is that the human immune system is extremely good at recognizing these engrafted organs as foreign and eliminating them. The immune system exhibits strategies in common with the nervous system, including complexity, diversity, and degeneracy. For years, scientists have attempted to identify which elements of the immune system cells are primarily involved in rejecting allografts with the aim of suppressing them. But what has been discovered is that there are numerous pathways via which a graft can be recognized and destroyed, so as in the example of the mythic hydra, when one successfully eliminates one immune pathway, another simply moves in to take its place.

What drives the rejection of the graft, arguably, is not a random set of receptors for foreign antigens but an image that recognizes foreignness. This is not the place to explain in detail how the immune system creates an internal image, but suffice it to say it is qualitatively similar to what was crudely explained for the nervous system. Nobel laureate Niels Jerne (1996), was the first to develop an elegant theory of idiotypic networks to explain how this is accomplished. Gerald Edelman, who also received a Nobel prize for his earlier work as an immunologist, was strategically prepared to adopt the lessons of the immune system to in the neurosciences. According to Edelman (2006), "Degeneracy is seen at many levels of biological organization, ranging from properties of cells up to those of language. It is an essential property of selectional systems, which would be likely to fail without it" (p. 33).

Promoting the Experiential Shift

What would tend to promote a catastrophic shift of the type that we are proposing? One answer is a reduction in the stress that may have contributed to the shift away from the normal attractor of self in the first place. With respect to the placebo response this might include a reduction in autonomic arousal or relaxation and factors that would tend to identify the original configuration of the self-attractor. These would tend to approximate the factors originally encoded during attachment, including a benevolent asymmetric doctor–patient relationship, empathic attunement, and meaning.

The proposed model is explanatory but obviously lacks detail. As currently configured, it is purely qualitative. However, it does hopefully succeed in placing the scientific emphasis where it belongs. In addition, there is precedence for successful theories in biology being purely qualitative (e.g., Darwinian evolution). In addition, the details of how placebo effects are mediated may at some level be beside the point. Obviously, different pathways would have to be selected to eliminate, for example, a headache versus a tumor. But if the homeostatic regulation of these diverse systems is as integrated as this theory suggests, it would not be necessary to select each system individually. Take an obvious example of what appears to be a simple yet complex response. Suppose that I want to move my hand. It is not necessary to describe every detail of how this is accomplished to understand the response. Ultimately, it is the image of what needs to happen that governs all of the required mechanistic activities. Evoking the placebo response may be comparable. The supraordinate response itself designates whatever is required to restore the core attractor of self.

What Is Explained, What Is Not

The foregoing model is consistent with certain empirical observations of the placebo response and predicts other elements that require testing:

(1) The placebo response is a shared human capacity determined by both innate and acquired factors.

(2) The potential to mount a placebo response is inherited as part of the primary neuronal repertoire, but its execution depends on information learned during early attachment and recalled within the therapeutic setting.

(3) As a nonlinear response, the development of placebo effects will be impossible to predict with accuracy.

(4) Sensitivity to initial conditions implies that a placebo responder on Monday may prove to be a nonresponder on Tuesday, even under similar circumstances. As an attractor-mediated response, recollecting some of the features of the self–attractor will suffice to restore it automatically.

(5) The degree of objective changes that can be achieved by the placebo response is probabilistically limited so that severe pathology would not generally be expected to be reversible.

(6) Disruptions in neural pathways that mediate and evaluate mind–body activities will limit placebo effects.

(7) The bipartite model of placebo effects may allow for reversion to background feeling states of well-being without objective changes in somatic physiology.

The heuristic value of a scientific theory is important, but only objective testing can establish or deny its accuracy. However, one reason why linear approaches have retained their popularity in the biomedical sciences is because most biomedical experiments yield few data points for analysis, which can make it difficult to establish nonlinearity. Approaches that yield large numbers of data points—for example, continuous physiological traces such as the electrocardiogram, electroencephalogram, and computer modeling of neural nets—are exceptions, and, not surprisingly, these have provided the source for most nonlinear advances in biology (Goldberger & West, 1987). But what can safely be concluded is that the complexity of the placebo response and virtually all other mind–body activities will not yield to traditional linear approaches.

It appears that the placebo response may be about to enter another phase in its circuitous history. Rather than as a mechanistically ineffective treatment or as a confounder of clinical trials, it may soon be accepted as a scientifically objective endogenous mode of healing rooted in nonlinear mind–body physiology. However, not all of the controversies that surround placebos are related to its science. Some are ethical issues. To address these, it is time to return to the realm of clinical practice.

7 Placebo and the Truth

Every man is fully convinced that there is such a thing as truth, or he would not ask any question.

Charles Sanders Pierce

Placebo and a Patient's Right to Know

The administration of a placebo raises ethical concerns. Physicians who knowingly prescribe placebos justify this deception by virtue of their good intentions of eliciting beneficial effects for the patient. But a patient who discovers that he or she has been deceived will likely find it difficult to trust a physician in the future. Sisela Bok (1974), a Harvard ethicist, had this to say:

> To forestall the individual and societal costs of placebos in patient care, deceptive prescription of placebos should be sharply curtailed. It should be undertaken only after careful diagnosis and consultation with colleagues in cases where there appears to be no other way out to attempt self-healing on the part of the patient. No active placebos should be prescribed; only ones known to be inert …. Most important, placebos should only be given out after careful consideration of non-deceptive ways to seek to stimulate "the will of being cured" (p. 23).

But what constitutes deception in practice is not always clear-cut. Consider the question of what and how much information should be shared with patients. Physicians are constantly faced with difficult therapeutic decisions, particularly when available therapies are likely of limited efficacy or entail the risk of substantial side effects, including death. Are they obligated to share such truths with their patients? Certainly, until recently, that was not the approach. In the 17th century, Jeremy Taylor (1660) counseled physicians to "lie like a doctor" if doing so might improve the patient's lot, and whereas much has changed since then, it is not certain that people's fundamental needs have. After all, if benevolent deception was therapeutically effective in the 17th century, why would it no longer be expected to be so in the 21st? In addition, if, as we have seen, placebo responses are learned in childhood, have their requirements changed substantially over the last 200 years? Would critics of withholding information advise sharing detailed medical information with a child? Whereas adults obviously have a greater capacity to process information and the right to know what will be done to them, it may be that placebo effects depend on the persistence of childhood gullibility.

Physicians H. Waitzkin and J. D. Stoeckle (1972) argued that the less uncertain the patient is concerning the elements of the decision-making process, the more likely that he or she will be willing to participate in it. The implication is that the democratic sharing of information is in the service of the treatment.

But a range of patient attitudes is encountered in clinical practice. There are patients who wish to defer to the opinions of their physicians. Like the taciturn patient encountered earlier in the present text, some resist being placed in positions where they are responsible for their medical decision making. When this is the case, should caregivers feel compelled to include these patients in the decision-making process?

The sharing of information is not neutral. I recently supervised a young doctor who was inclined to share her thoughts on diagnosis and treatment in detail with all of her patients. Her patients were made privy to the nuances of their disease, the vicissitudes of treatment, and the uncertainties of outcomes. I winced while listening to her inform elderly and confused patients about the side effects of their treatment, as many of them looked befuddled and frightened in response to this version of informed consent.

I suspect that this communication style is actually aimed more at containing this physician's anxieties than her patients'. Nevertheless, I was reticent to point this out, because from her perspective she was practicing with the prevailing attitude that patients must be fully informed about their condition and its treatment. By purposefully withholding information, one risks censure by colleagues as well as by the legal profession should a treatment go awry. But what is too often neglected in this approach is its possible negative impact on the placebo response and therapeutic outcome.

We have already seen evidence that telling the truth about a proposed intervention may detract from its efficacy when the truth is perceived as negative. Consider the study by Thomas (1987) in which 200 patients were given either positive or negative feedback from their physician with respect to their treatment options and were subsequently treated either with nothing or a placebo. The overall response rate in the group receiving positive feedback was greater than 60%, whereas negative commentary yielded responses in approximately 40% without any additional benefit observed for the co-administration of the placebo.

Any physician who has felt compelled to review the litany of potential side effects of a pill or a procedure with a patient knows how difficult it can be subsequently to evoke that patient's confidence concerning the treatment. So the physician is left in the precarious position of having to decide what his or her primary obligation is: sharing information to avoid culpability or assisting patients in getting well? Certainly, those critics who insist that full informational disclosure helps patients make informed choices and improves therapeutic outcome either have not adequately considered the spectrum of human nature or have not sufficiently considered the importance of placebo effects on therapeutic outcome. I would contend that what is primarily being ignored by the field of medicine is the fact that information critical to therapeutic outcome is primarily being evaluated by patients not by consciousness but at unconscious levels of processing. Certainly informed consent is an important ethical issue that bears consideration; however, there is little evidence that it resonates with human physiology. Controlled data will be required to determine whether informed consent actually more often promotes or detracts from therapeutic effects.

Unwitting Placebos

The ethical implications of prescribing a placebo depend on how one defines a placebo intervention. All would agree that choosing to prescribe a substance recognized as inactive—let us say a sugar pill—is a placebo intervention. But it could as well be concluded that administering a medication that has not been proven effective for the purpose for which it is being prescribed is also a placebo intervention. A review of the practices of physicians would undoubtedly uncover many instances of medications prescribed for purposes beyond what they were approved for. This practice also extends to administering drugs in schedules that have not been evaluated. Most doctors that I know in academic medicine, myself included, practice this way all the time.

Moerman (2002) pointed out that it is difficult to conclude that a placebo is inert when it yields objective effects. But what is actually implied is that a placebo has no known mechanism of action. Yet this idea is based on the misconception that the actions of most active drugs in the current pharmacopoeia are known. This is most assuredly not the case. Consider the following observation by Katz (1984):

> Why has the use of placebos been defended so apologetically and
> embarrassedly by their advocates and been attacked so vehemently by
> their opponents? That their use constitutes deceptive practice cannot
> be the whole answer.... Nor can the answer be found in the non-
> scientific basis of placebo treatments, for doctors continue to employ
> therapeutic agents such as steroids, chemotherapy, and antibiotics
> for many diseases, even though the scientific rationale for their use
> remains obscure (p. 190).

What then is the distinction between a placebo and an active
drug in which the mechanism is unknown? It is a good question
but without a good answer.

Practicing Therapeutics Outside the Box

As previously noted, the prescription practices of physicians are
rarely confined to the underlying proven efficacy of what is being
prescribed. Marcia Angell (2004), former editor of *New England
Journal of Medicine,* suggested that eliciting drug approval for
limited populations or for unrelated conditions is a strategy often
pursued by the pharmaceutical industry, as once a drug has been
approved it will often widely prescribed for purposes and populations of patients that it was not approved for. Physicians are too
busy to investigate the specific conditions of the U.S. Federal
Drug Administration (FDA) approval of new drugs and tend to
rely primarily on the medical literature, advertisements in medical journals, and drug promotions for this information.

Consider a recent example in which a combination antihypertensive drug was specifically tested in a population of African

Americans and was demonstrated to be more effective than placebo in the treatment of heart failure. The drug was approved by the FDA but only for use in this population. Does this drug also work in Caucasians, Asians, Native Americans, or Hispanics? The answer is that no one knows—and it is unlikely that the question will ever be critically evaluated, because once a drug has been approved it is virtually a certainty that physicians will opt to administer it for patients and conditions that are beyond its proven efficacy. The rational scientist in his laboratory is often a maverick when it comes to clinical care.

Other Considerations Concerning Placebos

Science and ethics are not the only areas of controversy that affect the administration of placebos. Katz (1984) had this to say:

> Recently, one of my students made the astute observation that the controversy over placebos brings to the surface more acutely and undeniably the discomfort physicians have generally experienced over the fact that the effectiveness of so many of their practices is strongly influenced by symbolic powers that reside in the silent laying on of hands and is not merely a result of their scientific treatments (p. 190).

Two uncomfortable truths that doctors often resist facing are the limited efficacy of what medicine actually has to offer and that much of what benefits patients may be placebo effects. There are large numbers of disorders for which current medical therapy currently provides limited benefits, including a host of incurable chronic diseases. Alternative medicine holds its greatest allure for patients with these disorders, but it also attracts those who are disenchanted with their physicians and with the side effects of the current pharmacopoeia.

A recent anecdote shared by a patient underscores this point. A youthful man in his early 50s was treated for mildly elevated blood pressure with a calcium-blocking agent. For several months, he complained of fatigue, lightheadedness, and heart palpitations. His doctor reassured him that his symptoms were unrelated to his medication. Nevertheless, he eventually chose to stop the medication—against his doctor's advice—after finding others with similar symptoms on an Internet chat room. Subsequently, he reported a sustained improvement in his disabling symptoms. Dissatisfied with traditional medicine, he consulted an herbal therapist for treatment, and his blood pressure has been well controlled.

Certainly, all drugs have potential side effects, and simply switching to another type of antihypertensive medication might have brought an end to his discomfort and controlled his hypertension as well. But this anecdote exemplifies how many patients become dissatisfied with traditional medical care and with medications that can produce more symptoms than they control.

There is a problem with traditional medicine's perspective on placebo effects. Why must effective drugs compete with placebo effects? It is one thing to demand that an active drug outperform a placebo yet another to denigrate what placebo effects have to offer. As therapeutic and placebo effects are inseparable, it is evident that this approach actually pits medicine against itself. Can physicians reclaim their comfort with placebos without compromising their status as medical scientists? I suggest that the answer is yes, but it will require elevating the placebo response to the level of science and no longer deprecating its importance.

Placebos and Randomized Controlled Trials

Some investigators have questioned the ethics of continuing to employ placebos in the evaluation of new therapeutic interventions. Rothman and Michels (2002) reviewed the value of including a placebo arm within a randomized controlled trial (RCT). The use of a placebo in the RCT is based on equipoise, which means that there is an a priori assumption of no difference between the test intervention and the placebo. The inclusion of a placebo arm in the RCT is critical for effective randomization. Randomization provides balance for a wide variety of variables, including those that have not been predetermined, so that the trial does not have to be overly restrictive with respect to its inclusion criteria. The placebo arm also facilitates blinding between the groups and the study investigators, which also reduces bias. The offer to treat facilitates an assessment of the placebo effects evoked by the RCT for both groups. But as Rothman and Michels point out, introducing any comparison arm that includes an offer of treatment can control for placebo effects.

Ethical considerations preclude subjecting patients to receiving a placebo when they are recognized to be an inferior mode of treatment. Problems with including a placebo arm also arise in the evaluation of new drugs for serious or life-threatening disorders, in which withholding a possibly effective treatment or falsely leading patients to believe that they may receive a new and possibly effective treatment are deemed unethical.

One way to avoid the inclusion of a placebo arm without sacrificing its value in trial design is to conduct an equivalence trial. However, this requires that an effective treatment must already exist for the disorder being investigated. The aim is to determine whether the new treatment is either an improvement—or at least no less effective—than what is currently available. As might be imagined, there are definite advantages to such an approach (Rothman & Michels, 2002). Above all, it allows the investigators to assess the efficacy of the new treatment head to head with a known treatment, an approach currently required by the FDA only in the testing of new antibiotics and chemotherapeutic agents.

Equivalence trials are large and costly, but their size makes the information retrieved from them more reliable. Furthermore, they protect patients from the unsuspected and untoward side effects of new drugs that may not be more potent than older drugs already recognized as safe. Consider the current controversy that surrounds the possible cardiac toxicity of COX-2 inhibitors, drugs that have never been proven more potent in the relief of arthritic pains than older drugs, including aspirin or ibu-profen, in which the side effects profiles were well established.

Patient Rights and Their Impact on the Science of Medical Therapeutics

From an ethical perspective, placebos should be avoided when their use potentially conflicts with the rights of the individual. The "Declaration of Helsinki" by the World Medical Association is the ethical standard via which the rights of the individual are to be upheld in the testing of new treatments. In 2000, the declaration was revised as follows:

> The benefits, risks, burdens, and effectiveness of a new method should be tested against those of the best current prophylactic, diagnostic, and therapeutic methods. This does not exclude placebo, or no treatment, in studies where no proven prophylactic, diagnostic, or therapeutic method exists.

The aim of this revision is clear: It affirms that the well-being of the individual must take precedence over competing interests. Although some have argued that individual rights are sufficiently protected by informed consent and by the decisions of internal review boards that oversee clinical investigation, the Helsinki declaration aims to exclude that level of decision making from the process. But the problems related to not including a placebo arm are also substantial. Placebos are required to demonstrate that a new treatment is effective when no other effective treatment exists. In the absence of a placebo control, clinicians may be repeatedly fooled by apparent therapeutic responses.

In response to the new and stricter criteria imposed on clinical trial design by the "Declaration of Helsinki" (World Medical Association, 2000), investigators have sought to define when it is still permissible to include a placebo arm in a clinical trial. Robert Levine (2002), a Yale bioethicist, suggested the following major criteria:

(1) When there is no existing therapy that is known to be at least partially effective
(2) When the risk of withholding a known effective treatment is judged to be exceedingly small

Having examined the placebo response from a variety of perspectives, the question that remains is can the placebo response be harnessed for its therapeutic benefits? And if it can, how does one maximize the likelihood of evoking it in practice?

8 The Challenge of Harnessing the Placebo Response

> "I think," said Mr. Dooley, "that if the Christyan Scientists had some science an' th' doctors more Christianity, it wudden't make anny diff'rence which ye called in—if ye had a good nurse.
>
> **Finley Peter Dunne (Mr. Dooley Says)**

Placebos in Practice

In a National Institutes of Health (NIH) conference on the science of placebo effects, a panel of investigators suggested that a primary goal of future placebo research should be to "operationalize the ability to elicit placebo responses in patients and then to identify the characteristics of practitioners who do this well" (Guess et al., 2002 p. 29).

Placebo responses are impossible to predict. No one has been successful in identifying placebo responders or in eliminating them from clinical trials. However, this does not mean that it is not possible to establish conditions that could promote the chances of eliciting placebo responses. Approaches aimed at optimizing placebo responses have centered on psychological and behavioral transactions between caregivers and patients. Moerman (2002) summarized the findings from salient studies demonstrating that physician beliefs, level of interest, concern for the patient, and communication style all influence the subsequent development of placebo effects.

In one study, attitudes expressed by doctors that included confidence, enthusiasm, affability, and the willingness to be reassuring were associated with the largest numbers of positive therapeutic responses (Uhlenhuth et al., 1966). By contrast, negative outcomes occurred when doctors were viewed as detached, persistently objective, or genuinely uncertain concerning the value of a drug being prescribed. The greatest negative outcomes were associated with doctors who were viewed as scientific in their approach.

The level of enthusiasm expressed by a clinician for a treatment is a sensitive issue. Unwarranted enthusiasm can detract from the scientific aims of medical practice. Clinicians who are judged to be excessive in their enthusiasm risk being labeled medicasters, charlatans, or quacks. Whereas these labels should be reserved for those who practice in bad faith, as medical historian Roy Porter (1989) pointed out in *On Quackery,* one rarely finds a physician who is willing to admit that his or her claims are nonvirtuous. Quacks are often masters at eliciting placebo effects so that it can be virtually impossible to distinguish their claims without the benefits of controlled trials.

In their review of the medical treatment of angina, Herbert Benson and David McCallie (1979) noted that a litany of drugs routinely that had been prescribed in practice prior to being formally evaluated in randomized clinical trials (RCTs) were generally accepted as therapeutically effective. The highest response rates (70–90%) were observed when enthusiastic doctors administered the drugs as compared with the lower response rates (30–40%) observed when the drugs were administered by physicians characterized as skeptical. However, these drugs failed to show any efficacy over placebos when rigorously examined.

Doctor as Placebo

What are the attitudes and approaches that enhance placebo responses? In a review in *American Journal of Family Practice*, medical practitioner Harold Brody (1997) suggested that focus should be directed primarily on the relationship between doctor and patient. He referred to the ideal mode of relationship as a sustained partnership that fosters trust and therapeutic alliance. According to Brody, the ideal physician exhibits the following qualities:

(1) Interested in the whole person

(2) Known to the patient over time

(3) Sensitive and empathic

(4) Reliable and trustworthy

(5) Willing to adapt medical goals to patient needs and values

(6) Encouraging of patient participation in health decision making

Communication: Is It What You Say or How You Say It?

Communication can promote or inhibit placebo effects. Striking an optimal balance is the art of therapy. Ideas communicated with limited affect can convey important information but can still limit the success of treatment. Conversely, communications laden with affects that fail to convey reassuring therapeutic information are also unlikely to be therapeutically effective.

Physicians can stand to learn a great deal from effective psychotherapists, whose training and practice have been focused on developing empathic styles of communication. Psychotherapists are keenly aware of the mutual influences therapist and patient exert on each other. Freud stressed the critical importance of transference–countertransference dynamics in analyzing how the interactions between patient and analyst were mutually influential. This area has since been explored in great detail and has yielded a plethora of theoretical stances emphasizing the complexities of interdependence (Meissner, 1996).

Klein (1986) recognized the uncanny way in which patients appear to influence the mental contents of their analysts subliminally by a process termed projective identification. In this dynamic, the analyst reports thoughts, feelings, and behaviors that are not part of his or her usual repertoire. It is easier to observe these influences in the isolation of the psychotherapeutic consulting room than in general medical practice, but they play out there as well. Consider the following example. A seasoned physician recognized for being painstakingly cautious in his diagnostic and therapeutic skills discovered that he had been unwittingly prescribing narcotics for a patient with a history of polysubstance drug abuse. When questioned by colleagues about how this happened, this generally thoughtful physician admitted that he had no idea why he had acted in this exceptional manner.

In a psychodynamic practice, supervisory colleagues would examine the factors that led to this apparent error in judgment. But innumerable examples of comparable uncharacteristic lapses in practice occur in medical practice and are never examined. Infant observation has demonstrated that humans communicate affect via subtle changes in facial expression and postural tone; however, it is by no means clear that these exchanges account entirely for the full range of subliminal communication. The idea of telepathic action at a distance does not jibe well with the expectations of modern science. But it is by no means impossible that humans have retained a primitive capacity to communicate telepathically, although what is likely being communicated are affects rather than facts. Whatever the actual modes of communication prove to be, it is undeniably true that communications influence the therapeutic dyad.

The Treatment Frame: Setting Up the Placebo Response

Another element of the therapeutic encounter that is often ignored is what psychotherapists refer to as the frame of the treatment. This includes the formal agreement as to when, where, and how often the participants will meet as well as the arrangements with respect to the fee and how payment will occur. Though these factors are all considered important in psychotherapies, only some apply routinely in medical practice.

The initial contact request for treatment may take place between the patient and a secretary, nurse, or clinic administrator. Ideally, these interactions should always be cordial and welcoming, but in practice this is not always the case. New patients may arrive at their appointment frustrated in response to difficulties that they have encountered in arranging a first appointment or in obtaining approval for the appointment by a third-party insurer. Although some might write off these inconveniences to daily adult life, they can set a negative tone for the visit and can limit placebo effects unless directly addressed. For this reason, it is good practice to inquire concerning, for example, possible difficulties in arranging an appointment, in traveling to the office, and in finding a parking space. This exhibition of concern may reverse the adverse consequences of these frustrations.

One may well question why such apparent trivialities are of consequence, but a seasoned psychotherapist would immediately recognize the answer, though it may escape others who have not been trained to be attuned to such matters. As was previously discussed in the section on attachment dynamics, mental representations develop on templates established in childhood. What might seem trivial to the adult mind can nevertheless resonate subliminally with the early schemata of childhood, leading to negative emotional responses that limit placebo effects.

Doctor as Caregiver: A Critical Factor in Harnessing Placebo Effects

Based on an increased awareness of the developmental interactions that promote placebo responses, the following interventions are proposed as likely to promote placebo responses. Whereas the current state of medical economics tends to limit the amount of time that can be spent with patients, all of what is suggested in this section can be achieved in a few minutes when a focused approach to the therapeutic transaction is adopted.

(1) Caregivers should be mindful of both nonverbal and verbal communications that can either foster or limit placebo responses. These include optimizing visual attunement, the appropriate introduction of physical

touch, and awareness of how facial expressions communicate approval, disapproval, confidence, or anxious concern.

(2) Caregivers should attempt to optimize physical distance in the room based on the level of comfort communicated either verbally or by body language. In response, the caregiver should be prepared to modify the seating positions in the examination or treatment room and to be attuned to how the patient responds to being touched.

(3) Ample time for history taking with focus on explication of chief complaints must be a standard part of the therapeutic situation. Concern, interest, and acceptance, should be conveyed via empathic listening.

(4) History taking should extend to past experiences with physicians, hospitals, and medications and should include any circumstances that may color the patient's symptoms.

The importance of eye contact, verbal cues, and touch is based on how mind–body activities are modulated in early affect transactions between infant and caregiver. They contribute to what Winnicott (1960) termed the holding environment. The recapitulation of these behaviors is purposefully aimed at evoking the implicit recall of early states of well-being.

Visual attunement and gaze mirroring are critical in development. Self-psychologists have emphasized the importance of mirroring in the healthy development of self-construct and as a pathway toward the optimal development of empathy. Interestingly, neuroscientists have recently identified groups of neurons in the human brain that appear to play a role in how mirroring is physiologically achieved.

In 1995, Italian neuroscientists Iacommo Rizzolati and Vittorio Gallase discovered that neurons in the ventral premotor area of macaque monkeys are activated whenever a monkey performs a complex action. Most of these neurons are directly involved in mediating motor activities. However, Rizzolati and Gallese discovered that a subset is activated even when the monkey is only watching another monkey perform the same activities. These scientists concluded that these mirror neurons were not merely involved in confirming the adage, "Monkey see, monkey do," but were also critical in allowing the observer to place himself or herself into the position of an individual being observed (Rizzolati and Craighero, 2004).

Subsequently, functional magnetic resonance imaging (fMRI) researchers at the University of California, Los Angeles (Iacoboni et al., 2005) showed that cells in the human anterior cingulate gyrus were activated in a subject who watched another subject being poked by a needle. This empathic connection serves to dissolve the barrier between self and other, thereby allowing one to vicariously experience another's perspective—that is, to experience another empathically.

During the first year of life, gaze interactions and attuned facial expressive transactions between the mother and infant are of paramount importance in fostering affect regulation. Infants smile in response to seeing the enlarged pupils of a caregiver and in turn exhibit papillary dilatation. Stern (1985) referred to this as the mutual regulatory system of arousal that mediates mind–body well-being. For these reasons, attuned visual transactions are likely to promote placebo responses. How eye contact is established can convey important clues to the patient's underlying level of comfort with previous caretakers and strangers. The inability to sustain eye contact or the exhibition of a purposefully aversive gaze tends to disrupt attunement and may limit placebo effects.

Verbal communications should be aimed at two distinct levels of the patient's mental function. The first is word based and aims at communicating factual narrative information that promotes shared meaning between patient and doctor. Language targets the higher cortical activities of the left brain and is important in promoting meaning and other higher cortical symbolic functions. But as critical is prosody: the volume, tone, and rhythm of spoken communication. We are all well acquainted with the evocative nature of poetry, which accents both the prosodic and metaphoric features of language. Prosody evokes responses primarily from the right brain and strongly influences the limbic system. Infant observation suggests that the prosody of vocalizations synchronizes affectual responses between mother and infant—often as cooing—and is itself a highly effective method of soothing.

It follows from this that authoritative explanations of the patient's disorder and outlines of possible treatments are unlikely to evoke placebo effects if they are perceived as delivered in harsh, haughty, or affectless tones that lack the qualities of prosody established during childhood. Even seasoned clinicians are at times reticent to recognize that style is as important as content in determining the therapeutic outcome.

When I was a medical student, one of my professors cautioned that no therapeutic encounter is complete until the physician has laid hands on the patient. Touch is one of the areas that distinguishes psychological from somatic treatments. The practice of healing touch is ancient. As recently as the 17th century, it was believed that being touched by the king of England could heal scrofula, a tuberculous infection of the lymph nodes (Shapiro & Shapiro, 1997). Modern faith healers continue to effect their healing by touching the faithful.

In a recent fMRI study, researchers examined the beneficial effects of direct touch on perceived threat (Coan, Schaefer, and Davidson, 2006). They examined 16 married women who were subjected to an electric shock while either holding their husbands' hands or the hands of anonymous male experimenters or with no hand holding. The results showed the greatest attenuation in activation of neural systems associated with threat while holding a spouse's hand, with smaller observed responses while holding the hand of a stranger, and no attenuation in the absence of hand holding. Interestingly, the degree of attenuation on spousal hand-holding also varied directly with the reported quality of the marital relationship. These results support an important role for physical touch in reducing levels of perceived stress and provide evidence for the role of touch in some observed placebo effects.

Whereas the role of physical and sexual abuse in a sizable percentage of patients seeking psychological treatment argues against adopting touch as a therapeutic element under most circumstances, it is an indispensable factor in establishing a holding environment, as the term suggests, and is an essential part of the therapeutic encounter in somatic medicine. Appropriate touch diminishes autonomic arousal. A cursory physical examination may leave other patients feeling deprived of the soothing effects of being touched. A careful history should determine whether touch is likely to be interpreted as soothing or intrusive.

Something to Keep in Mind: How Do I Look to Others?

It is important for the physician to gain insight into how he appears to others. Relatively few of us are conscious of how facial expressions and postures effectively communicate feelings. A dour appearance may convey serious-mindedness, but it can also impede the relaxation of an anxious patient, who may be seeking a more welcoming countenance. Facial expressions can convey boredom or distaste and understandably detract from placebo effects. Though most of us are not practiced in being mindful of how we appear to others, this can be achieved by mentally attending to one's facial expression during the therapeutic encounter. It is recognized that consciously formulating the facial musculature into a smile can evoke pleasurable affects both in oneself and in others. Slouching in one's chair or fidgeting with a writing instrument communicate inadequate concern for the patient.

Don't Just Do Something—Sit There[*]

Physicians tend to place a high priority on action, which is precisely the opposite of what psychotherapists hold to be important. Clearly, each has its role. Physicians view listening as the prelude to action, as the medical history is obtained prior to conducting a physical examination and formulating a therapeutic intervention. But what may not be appreciated is that listening can by itself be therapeutic. My psychologist colleagues Anne Alonso and Scott Rutan (1996) emphasized the therapeutic benefits of empathic listening coupled with inaction.

Many patients come to their physician with the primary desire to be heard and understood. For some, the doctor's office

---

[*] Reported to have been Adlai Stevenson's advice to President John Kennedy during the Cuban Missile Crisis.

is the only place where they can expect to be afforded any positive attention. For this reason, doctors must be willing to give patients, within reason, ample time to convey their stories. They should be interrupted as little as possible and then only to obtain clarification. The failure to listen is the most common complaint voiced by disgruntled patients. Despite more demands on time than ever before, listening is an essential part of the therapeutic process; it is not a luxury.

Active listening includes a variety of elements that promote attunement. These include attention and efforts at internally recreating the mental and physical states of the patient. These are conveyed via the patient's facial expressions, tone of voice, patterns and depth of ventilation, and postures. Active listening contributes to organizing the patient's mind–body states. The failure to listen appropriately may be sensed as abandonment and may limit the placebo response.

Try Taking a Placebo History

Optimal history taking should address elements of the patient's history that potentially affect placebo responsiveness. This may be conveyed during the course of the patient's narrative but may require more active exploration. It is commonplace for pediatricians and psychiatrists—but not other physicians—to take an early developmental history. As placebo responses are rooted in early development, this aspect of the patient's history should be addressed. This includes inquiring into perinatal medical and social history, pediatric diseases, hospitalizations, early parental deprivation, and major physical and emotional traumas.

Questions should be asked concerning medication use, not only with respect to the list of current medication but also regarding attitudes that surround the taking of medications. A large number of patients have adverse attitudes toward medications—some based on previous experience with drug side effects and others reflecting irrational fears of dependence or even paranoid fears of being poisoned.* Certainly, knowing this will influence placebo outcomes. As always, it is important to inquire into current social situations, including family illnesses, illnesses, and deaths that may be contributing to the patient's interpretation of his or her symptoms.

Brody (1997) suggested that physicians should be willing to work together with patients in constructing the narrative of their illness, its root cause, its present meaning, and implications for future recovery. This should, of course, include a deeper investigation into how patients understand the medical interventions that are being offered as well as their hopes and concerns. Brody, writing primarily for primary care physicians, recognized that this group may be best positioned to engage in these kinds of exercises with long-term patients. In summary, a variety of methods can be adopted in the service of evoking placebo responses,

---

* In my experience, this is actually quite common and is often guised by an emphasis on wanting to be natural.

Table 8.1   Therapeutic Behaviors That May Promote Placebo Effects

Asymmetric power dynamic between doctor and patient
Physical proximity
Empathic attention
Good listening skills
Gaze attunement
Appropriate touch
Communication style (language and prosody)
Welcoming physical appearance

but practitioners must be cognizant of the fact that they are neither foolproof nor fully reliable, due to the nature of the placebo response.

Placebo and Complementary or Alternative Medicine: Persistent Doubts

It seems fitting to conclude this text with a discussion of the role of the placebo response in alternative and complementary practices. The history of medicine has been an ongoing dialectic between differing strands of practice, each rooted in its own theoretical framework. Since the Enlightenment, the dominant element in the conversation in the West has been allopathic medicine, which aims at grounding medical diagnosis and therapeutics in scientific experimentation. This mode of medicine eschews metaphysical arguments and tends not to involve itself with a priori concepts or teleology.

Although one might expect that its dominance of medical practice would be overwhelming, in truth this is not—and has never been—the case. Instead, claims by alternative healing sects, often with disparate orientations, have always tended to counter scientific rationalism. Their continued popularity does not reflect merely an antagonism towards science but is attributable, in part, to a substantial measure of therapeutic success.

Alternative medicine is not a monolithic enterprise. It is a pluralistic endeavor, as Porter (1997 p. 390) noted in his description of alternative practices in the 19th century:

> Some were religious, others secular; some favored science, others folk wisdom; some glamorized the heroic prophet, others made every man his own doctor—but typically they shared some common ground. They tended to denounce modern lifestyles as unnatural and accused regular medicine of being an oligarchic closed shop, an obscurantist racket devoted to self-aggrandizement.

Although the alternative movements had substantial followings in the United States—which has always enjoyed a certain maverick reputation among nations—their inspiration was rooted in Germany. Samuel Hahnemann—the 18th-century father of homeopathy, one of the leading alternatives to allopathic medicine—argued that there were three possible approaches to healing: (1) prevention; (2) the allopathic method that he labeled palliative and potentially harmful; and (3) homeopathy, in which patients were treated by the principles of similarities (i.e., that like cures like) and with infinitesimals, the extremely small amounts of drugs Hahnemann believed were more effective than the larger amounts administered in allopathic practice. The guiding principles of these alternative systems were either that God or the body itself held the key to healing, a notion that we have previously encountered in ancient societies. The proper role of the physician in alternative medicine is not to interfere with nature.

According to Bodekker and Kronenberg (2002 p. 1582), up to 70% of people in the West, where alternative practices have largely been relegated to a liminal position in the medical arena, continue to avail themselves of what these practices have to offer. Despite the fact that Americans are less likely than Europeans and Canadians to choose an alternative mode of treatment, the annual expenditure on these practices in the United States is staggering, approximately $15 billion a year in the late 1990s despite the fact that their therapeutic claims have not been scientifically established (Watkins & Lewith, 1997). In fact, their premises have often been viewed by allopathic medicine as so far beyond the pale of science as not to be worthy of either the time or the effort required to test them.

It took an increased awareness of the economic impact of these approaches and direct pressure by some members of Congress, who along with their families regularly availed themselves of these approaches, to induce the NIH to create an Institute of Complementary/Alternative Medicine for the express purpose of examining their efficacy by scientific methods. The problem has been where to put the effort, time, and money, as the list of recognized modes of alternative practice compiled by the Office of Alternative Medicine numbers in the hundreds. It includes the commonly used practices of chiropractic, acupuncture, osteopathy, and homeopathy and ranges the gamut to include approaches such as reflexology, massage therapy, Aryuvedic medicine, macrobiotic diets, herbs, blue light treatment, and crystal therapies, to name only a few. Some would opt also to include music therapy, dance therapy, and psychotherapy as alternative unproven techniques. All of these approaches have their devotees, and they are often supported by certificate training programs as well as by their own journal publications.

Some approaches such as relaxation techniques or mindfulness meditation are undoubtedly beneficial, as they promote subjective states of well-being and reproducible physiological changes. Herbert Benson (1996) argued that mind–body medicine should be separated from other alternative therapies, and this may be a sound idea. However, mind–body medicine has also made claims that far exceed what has been proven. For example, although the relaxation response can diminish anxiety, there is little or no objective evidence that it promotes immune responses, at least not by the schedules touted by those who promote its beneficial medical effects (Kradin & Benson, 2000). Unfortunately, too many mind–body practitioners tend to adopt the position that stress is universally bad, with little evidence to support this broad claim.

The facts actually show something quite different. The diversity of human responses is such that the same stressor may be converted into a potentially adverse response (e.g., hypertension) in some but not in others. In addition, a certain amount of stress actually promotes learning and efficiency without any undue effects. In some subjects a stressor can lead to sympathetic nervous system arousal and activation of the hypothalamic-pituitary-adrenal (HPA) axis with the release of cortisol, and when stress is repetitive and chronic the long-term effects may be deleterious. Esther Sternberg (2001) suggested this as a factor in the pathogenesis of the chronic fatigue syndrome, as patients with this disorder appear to develop diminished cortisol production in response to stress. It has certainly been my experience that the vast majority of patients with this disorder have histories of high levels of stress and achievement prior to burning out. But many others show little propensity to react this way. Furthermore, what some perceive as stress appears to have little somatic consequence, as evidenced by the inability to detect concomitant physiological changes. Yet when I have lectured on stress at mind–body conferences attended by the public, I have frequently encountered incredulity about suggesting that there is little evidence that stress is globally bad or relaxation is universally good.

The issues raised by nontraditional therapies such as acupuncture or energy healing are more complex, as these approaches are based on worldviews that are considerably different from those encountered in the West (Kaptchuk, Edwards, & Eisenberg, 1996). Western medicine views structure and function as inextricable. It is an essential Newtonian viewpoint, and in most circumstances it is fundamentally sound. For example, if a nerve in the arm is severed, a competent neurologist can accurately predict the consequent sensorimotor deficit with little error, and no other scientific approach is required. But contrast this perspective with that expressed within the Buddhist *Heart Sutra* (Pine, 2004), in which it is suggested that both form and structure are empty. Eastern medicine adopts ideas based on views of reality that are both subjective and focused on unconventional scales.

Few in the West would doubt that an oak table is substantial, even though we know scientifically speaking that it is made up mostly of space with some atomic constituents. But from the point of view of certain Eastern philosophies, the table is empty and lacks substance. Medical anatomy in Eastern traditions often bears little resemblance to that in the West, as even a cursory examination of the standard acupuncture meridians confirms (Figure 8.1). In addition, the dominant perspectives in Eastern medical traditions focus on restoring balance and wholeness, an approach that is closer to the ancient Greek idea of humoral imbalance than to that currently held by modern allopathic medicine.

The point is that not only are the techniques of many alternative approaches different than those practiced in the West, but their worldview is also unlike our own. It is questionable whether one can pick and choose approaches from different traditions and interpolate them into a substantially different worldview and

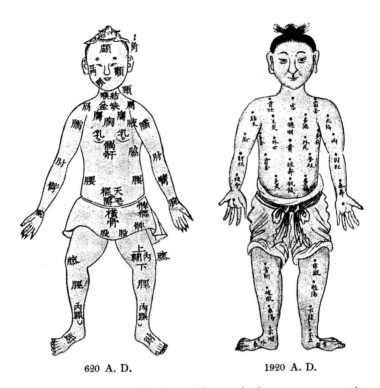

620 A. D.   1920 A. D.

Figure 8.1 Acupuncture Meridians. The standard acupuncture meridians have changed little in hundreds of years. These have no correlation with the anatomic pathways of nerves recognized by Western medicine.

system of therapeutics. The issues raised by alternative medicine are not limited to whether or not they may be effective; they extend to the heart of our Western beliefs.

Despite seemingly inexhaustible testimonials by adherents, with few exceptions (Kaptchuk, Edwards, & Eisenberg, 1996) when alternative approaches have been examined in RCTs, they have not shown efficacy beyond placebos. The one exception may be homeopathy: A meta-analysis published in the *Lancet* claimed that this method was superior to placebo (Linde & Clausis, 1997), but despite the fact that the study appeared to be well done, its results were not generally accepted. This speaks to an important criterion of science: What is being claimed must make sense within the domain of what is already known. The idea of infinitesimal dilutions of a drug being effective has no recognized basis in physical or biochemical science. Rather than reject all of the current tenets of these sciences, the medical community preferred to conclude that the study was somehow flawed, an eminently reasonable conclusion.

In other instances where clinical trials have actually purported to establish the benefits of an alternative approach, the claims have not withstood critical analysis. For example, an RCT showing that chiropractic medicine was more effective than the reading of a pamphlet failed to control for the critical element of human contact in the placebo control. Proponents of alternative and complementary medicine counter that Western scientific methods diminish the specific efficacy of these approaches by interfering with subjective experience or by interfering with energy fields. Adherents of alternative approaches often express little interest in scientific methods, as they do not support their beliefs.

It is not my aim to argue whether alternative modes of medical practice are true or false. As William James (1904) concluded, radical empiricism cannot establish or deny the truth of another's experience. If one believes that an alternative approach is effective, no one can prove him or her wrong. But from the perspective of Western science, most—if not all—alternative approaches have failed to demonstrate beneficial effects beyond those attributable to the placebo response.

Despite this, there has been an increasing trend within academic medical centers to offer a range of alternative therapeutic modalities to their patients. This largely reflects their recognition that there are economic benefits to getting on board the alternative medicine bandwagon and that there are potentially sizable losses in failing to do so. But in embracing alternative approaches, these centers also grant them an imprimatur of scientific legitimacy. Furthermore, these programs are often headed up by physicians or other health professionals who have abandoned the rigors of the scientific method and are often motivated by personal beliefs that are substantially different from those of their academic medical colleagues or are motivated by personal gain.

Whereas it is never wise to begrudge an individual his or her beliefs, it may be equally unwise for credible academic institutions to support these endeavors without first insisting on evidence of their scientific efficacy. Some academics have concluded that alternative methods may not be effective but that they also are harmless. But this is not entirely true because as Evans (2004) noted, "Potentially toxic levels of arsenic and cadmium have been found in homeopathic preparations, for example, and the use of acupuncture needles have led to the transmission of diseases such as HIV and hepatitis B" (p. 142).

As an astute critic once commented, there is no such thing as alternative medicine; instead, there is medicine that has been proven effective in its own right versus treatments that rely exclusively on the placebo response. There are legitimate concerns that the scientific advances made by Western medicine could, if not guarded, slide back into what Sigmund Freud referred to as the "black mud of occultism" (Ferris, 1998 p. 289).

As previously noted, patients with chronic disorders that respond poorly to conventional medical interventions are the primary consumers of alternative medical approaches. The lack of therapeutic success with these patients strains the limit of the mainstream therapeutic dynamic. Frustrated and often ill-prepared to face the implications of helplessness, some clinicians withdraw emotionally and physically from patients with incurable diseases, leaving a vacuum to be filled by other approaches that might offer relief. Alternative medicine practitioners are inclined to focus their time and effort on these patients, adopting attitudes and behaviors that are more likely to be favorable in evoking the placebo response. Unfortunately, it appears that the specific techniques they proffer have little to offer beyond this admittedly substantial contribution. But society needs practitioners who are adept at evoking placebo responses. The optimal therapeutic approach integrates these capacities with those that can provide additional benefits beyond placebo effects. How to achieve this is the challenge. Until traditional medicine confronts the problem and adopts a more favorable stance toward placebo effects, alternative medicine will continue to fill a niche.

It is possible that some alternative approaches may at some point in the future actually prove more effective than placebo. Should that be the case, within reason, medical science will have to investigate how they act. But until that time, there is abundant evidence to conclude that most of the claims made by alternative medicine should be ignored. Instead, what should be intensively investigated is how placebo responses develop.

When All Is Said and Done, Where Do Things Stand?

The story of the placebo response has taken us along a long and winding road. At its end, hopefully the reader has been convinced that the placebo response is an important factor in therapeutics that merits intensive scientific investigation. From my perspective, there may be no more urgent problem in medicine than establishing how placebo effects are generated. Yet in the 21st century, one is still hard pressed to identify more than a handful of medical scientists who are actively exploring the mechanism of placebo action. The following is a final brief account of why this is the case. It deserves repeated emphasis, as it is doubtful that resistance will be overcome until the contributing factors are recognized and addressed.

Table 8.2 Reasons Medical Scientists Resist Accepting the Importance of the Placebo Effects

Limited well-controlled data

Educational deficits with respect to the placebo response

Specialty training of physicians

Antagonism of pharmaceutical industry

Lack of interest in matters psychological

Emphasis on Newtonian science

Narcissistic vulnerabilities (placebo envy)

Scientific Subspecialization

The current training in most medical schools does not adequately prepare physicians or medical scientists to consider all of the pertinent elements of neurobiology, psychology, and physiology that contribute to the development of the placebo response. Psychiatrists are cognizant of the difficulties, but they are insufficiently trained in medical issues to make a serious impact in that arena. Few are prepared to cross scientific disciplines in sufficient depth to address complex mind–body interactions like the placebo response.

Multiple questions concerning the placebo response require investigation. The neurophysiological pathways of the response should be elucidated along with the neurotransmitters that are primarily responsible for mediating it. Efforts should be made to determine whether concomitant changes in electroencephalography, electrocardiography, or ventilatory and blood pressure traces indicate system linkages that may be governed by deterministic chaos in response to a placebo. Although most humans likely have the capacity to generate a placebo response, there may be exceptions. The rates of placebo responses in a host of disorders should be examined to determine the physiological limits of the response.

Once the mechanisms of the placebo response have been elucidated, it might be possible to promote well-being and healing via both behavioral and pharmacological interventions that promote this response. This could see the emergence of a whole new arena of ancillary psychotropic for disease. The possibilities and potential benefits from such research are staggering. It might one day be possible to develop a drug that blocks placebo effects, and this would greatly assist in evaluating the specific actions of new drugs without contamination by placebo effects. Surely such a project might interest the pharmaceutical industry, yet few currently share my enthusiasm; why is this the case?

The Pharmaceutical Industry Has a Fixed and Negative Attitude About the Placebo Response

The bureaucracy within the pharmaceutical industry is enormous. As Marcia Angell (2004) suggested, novel ideas are far less prevalent in the industry than the public realizes. The industry is highly conservative and takes few risks. It tends to favor patentable sequels based on minor changes in drugs that are already known to be effective. From its perspective, the only drug with respect to the placebo response that they might be interested in is one that makes it disappear. This is understandable, as corporate profits are hindered by placebo effects. Yet without pharmaceutical industry support, it will be difficult to generate enthusiasm for promoting scientific interest in the placebo response.

The Narcissistic Vulnerabilities of Physicians Who Refuse to Admit the Possibility That Much of What They Have to Offer Is the Result of Good Interpersonal Skills Rather Than Scientific Expertise

When the placebo response is raised as a topic with many academic physicians and scientists, one can watch as their eyes glaze over. Why is it that the potentially most exciting aspect of healing evokes so little enthusiasm from professionals sworn to the practice of healing? There is no one answer to this question.

I dare say that most physicians have not fully considered the implications of the placebo response. I do not believe that most are aware that it is inseparable from other therapeutic effects. There is a curious tendency to think of placebo effects as *other*. Even in RCTs there is a persistent misconception on the part of some to believe that drug effects and placebo effects sort out with whether one is in the drug arm or placebo arm of the trial rather than the recognition that drug effects are the sum of drug- and placebo-response activities. My interests have included mind–body interactions for some time, but until

relatively recently I had not given the subject much thought—
so failure to educate is certainly part of the problem.

In addition, there is an entrenched belief among physicians
that mind–body interactions are not only imaginal but also
truly imaginary. This reflects the emphasis of materialistic philosophy within the sciences. There is an inclination to dismiss
mind as immaterial and as a factor in physical disease. Mind
only becomes a legitimate area of research, from this perspective,
when first reduced to the materiality of the brain. This may not
be the case for psychologists, but it is a common attitude among
somatic physicians. Their lack of expertise and interest in psychological matters have thwarted investigations into mind–body
interactions. Even psychiatrists, who as a group have become
increasingly biological in their approach over the last 25 years
may give matters of mind short shrift. A well-known psychiatric
colleague of mine who works in the area of psychological trauma
once expressed to me that there was no such thing as a psychosomatic disorder.

But it is evident, as it was to René Descartes, that the mind is
distinct from the brain. Although the mind is dependent on the
brain, it is also an emergent phenomenon that cannot be reduced
to the nervous system per se. Mind wields substantial influence
over the entire body, as Cannon (1942) showed in extreme form
in the cases of voodoo death. However, scientists prefer and
choose to limit their sphere to the five senses; that is, they address
the material world sensationally—exactly what cannot be done

with mind. Furthermore, few physicians give credence to the unconscious processes that mediate the placebo response.

For some physician scientists there is a genuine concern of practicing outside of the safety and support of one's colleagues. This is a legitimate worry. When I declared my own interests in mind–body interactions, many of my medical colleagues expressed surprise, amusement, or contempt. This area was not considered a proper mode of study and was too far removed from their medical interests. Yet those who are interested must strive against resistance to remain under the umbrella of medical orthodoxy. It does the field no good when one chooses to turn one's back on medical orthodoxy to preach to the choir. Within mind–body and alternative and complementary circles, investigators too often lose the critical perspective that is necessary to conduct rigorous research, further compounding the problem.

I believe that there is yet another explanation for the lack of interest in the placebo response, and here I put on my psychoanalytical hat. Imagine training most of your life to master the scientific tools of your profession. This means years of studying anatomy, physiology, pharmacology, pathology, and clinical technique, all preceded by a strong premedical university education in the basic sciences. Next, imagine being told that much of what you have to offer therapeutically has little to do with what you know and more to do with how you behave and that someone with good interpersonal skills might be as effective as you are as a healer.

Physicians are right to be proud of their education and what they have to offer. But all of their education and skill pales to some degree in the face of countless millions of years of natural evolution. The mind–brain is an extraordinary organ that has transformed the world but it is itself the product of nature. The placebo response is also a force of nature. Many doctors in the West are imbued with the heroic inclination to overcome nature in their quest to cure disease. Might it not be better to find ways of cooperating with the placebo response rather than to continue dismissing it contemptuously out of what is (reader, please excuse the quip) placebo envy? The human ego, as the Greek playwrights well recognized, is in constant threat of being overcome by forces greater than itself. One can choose to confront nature with envy, humiliation, and rage or, alternatively, like Job, recognize where man stands in the greater scheme of things.

Failure of the Academic Medical System to Reward Good Doctoring Skills

Most medical school curricula offer courses on the art of medicine, and in the current age of political correctness interpersonal dynamics has received increased attention. The focus of academic medicine is most often on what brings in money, although it can be effectively argued that what actually brings in the money is good patient care, which includes facility with evoking the placebo response. But what drives academics and academic promotion is often research, so that some of the finest clinicians who have little inclination to be researchers are never represented among the academic medical staff. I would not have secured a position at the Harvard hospital where I have practiced now for nearly 30 years had I not been actively working successfully in a research lab.

In many respects this arrangement is appropriate. One of the major aims of academic medicine is research, as without it little progress could be made in medicine. However, over the years I have seen many talented humane clinicians passed over for positions or alternatively awarded academic positions that are dead ends with respect to promotion. This may be changing, as it becomes increasingly difficult to procure government funding for research. But suffice it to say that most academic centers have not been primarily interested in hiring good "placebo-response evokers."

The Failure of Medical Science to Adopt Nonlinear Analysis to the Investigation of Complex Systems Like the Nervous System

The placebo response is distinguished by its unpredictability and currently lacks an explanatory mechanism. The fundamental tenets of medical science are Newtonian. Practically speaking, Newtonian science is what was learned in high school physics, chemistry, and biology. It is based on descriptions of the material world; that is, it is empirically based and includes the premise of linear causality, comparable to the example of the billiard balls discussed in chapter 1.

In his momentous work *The Structure of Scientific Revolutions,* Thomas Kuhn (1970) described how a crisis in scientific confidence may arise when an anomalous phenomenon appears that cannot be adequately described by the prevailing paradigm. Luckily, the recent development of chaos theory to explain the nonlinear behavior of complex systems may prove applicable to explaining phenomena like placebo effects

The scientific myth has many premises and ramifications. In it, objectivity dominates, and subjectivity is often devalued or ignored. The objects of observation, including patients, are reduced, as philosopher Martin Buber suggested, to things in an I–it relationship (Buber & Smith, 1950).This approach fails to recognize the individual beyond the disease, as evidenced by the tendency for some physicians to refer thoughtlessly to patients as, for example, the cirrhotic in room 410 or the appendectomy on the operating room schedule. Reductionist science relies on an atomistic approach, in which the fundamentals of things are reduced to smaller and smaller units. The critical method of analysis, when applied to the psyche, is often experienced as just that: critical. As a result, as the research of Thompson showed (2005), a scientific attitude that fosters the I–it perspective is antithetical to the type of holding environment necessary to foster the placebo response.

Modern biological science shuns complexity, particularly as the latter is viewed as a possible impediment to translating basic scientific observations rapidly into therapeutic action. The progress of reductionistic medical science has been and continues to be impressive, and this mode of analysis will undoubtedly continue to have a dominant place in medical experimentation. But its scope is also limited. When I first worked as a research fellow in an immunology laboratory, I learned that certain bioassays could be applied only along the linear portion of their standard curves. In reality, bioassays yield S-shaped sigmoid curves, but scientists ignore this fact to establish a range of points along the linear portion of the curve. Strategies of approximation, rounding off, and ignoring nonlinearity can seem pragmatic. But as meteorologists, chemists, and other physical scientists have come to realize, there is a world of phenomena to be explored scientifically that can no longer be erroneously attributed to noise. Metaphorically speaking, it is time to explore the outer edges of the curve.

Finally, like the psychosomatic symptom, there appears to be something in the placebo response that is intent on defying explanation. As Bootzin and Caspi (2002) emphasized, the phenomenology of placebo responses is metastable, and much of what is known about it reveals its mercurial characteristics:

> This is particularly the case when one examines the elements that have evoked the placebo response at different times in its history. They [placebo responses] evolve and change in response to biological and

psychological signals that play a role in the therapeutic process.... The placebo effect always interacts to an unpredictable degree with other elements of the therapeutic intervention.... Albeit methodologically very complex and difficult to test, the interaction implies that even in experimental arms of randomized controlled trials the placebo effect may account for some of the outcome we measure (p. 126).

Via the retrospectoscope, it is easy for modern man to be astounded by the apparent naïveté of patients and doctors in the past. Few sophisticated present-day urban dwellers would be expected to benefit from, for example, eye of newt, as they might have prior to Shakespeare's time. Yet most of us are easily convinced that modern placebo interventions such as arthroscopic surgery or antidepressant medication ought to be effective.

However, rationality is not the only factor that promotes placebo effects. Consider the continued popularity of dietary supplements, nutriceuticals, and alternative medicine treatments, none of which has been proven to be beneficial. One might be tempted to conclude that irrational elements can also trigger placebo effects. These elements may persist from earlier times in psychological development, like the magical stage of childhood thinking described by developmental psychologist Jean Piaget. The persistence of magical thinking may explain the persistent appeal that certain exotic treatments hold for some members of society. Some of my colleagues are medical scientists and wear copper bracelets for their arthritis or sit in front of light sources to treat their depression, with no sense of contradiction.

In the future, medicine will certainly come to appreciate the indivisibility of mind–body. One day, all of the parts of the body will be recognized as inseparable and dependent on one another. Science will shift back from the molecular realm to reexplore how organisms function as a whole. The placebo response, like the weather, may be fundamentally unpredictable but it too will be known.

The placebo response is evidence that we are both all related yet unique. The mixed, shared and idiosyncratic elements of placebo effects are yet another reflection of this paradox. Medical science will have to come to grips with this paradox in the future, as no single drug, surgery, psychotherapy, or doctor will ever fit all. Though medical science, still steeped in a myth of omnipotence, may attempt to force Procrustean solutions on the sick, it will not succeed.

Carl Jung viewed neurosis as the failed tyranny of the logical mind over the requirements of human physiology. Despite the marvelous achievements of the human mind, it is limited by other elements of its nature. As artist Paul Gauguin recognized in his most famous painting (1897), it is important to know *D'où venons-nous? Que sommes-nous? Où allons-nous?* (What are we? Where do we come from? Where we are going?) We are a special class of mammals called primates. We have evolved over millions of years from simpler forms of life in response to sets of natural laws. Our physical limits, biologically determined needs, and behaviors are largely beyond our volition. It is one thing to investigate these limitations and in the future attempt to modify them, but it is quite another to ignore them. The latter is a recipe for failure, largely in the form of dis-ease.

The current emphasis on self-help may be in the spirit of the American puritanical tradition and to some extent is within the spectrum of our optimal physiology. But as mammals, we are innately social animals. The evolved systems of healing have incorporated this fact. Self-help in the extreme tends to ignore and deny this fact and as such finds little solid scientific support. Instead, everywhere one looks in the mammalian world, one encounters evidence of mutuality and interdependence that begins necessarily at the level of neonatal attachment. Ultimately, we must heed the advice of the oracle at Delphi: Know thyself! But I would hasten to add that we must know others as well, as that is the true path to healing.

Bibliography

Aboud, L. (2004, June 18). Drug makers to bar "placebo responders" from drug trials. *The Wall Street Journal.*

Ader, R. (1997). The role of conditioning in pharmacotherapy. In A. Harrington (Ed.), *The placebo effect: An interdisciplinary exploration* (pp. 138–165). Cambridge, MA: Harvard University Press.

Alonso, A., & Rutan, S. (1996). Don't just do something, sit there! *Behavioral Science, 20,* 43–55.

American Psychiatric Association (2000). *Diagnostic and statistical manual (DSM)-IV, revised (TR).* Washington, DC: APA.

Anderson, J. A., & Rosenfeld, E. (Eds.). (1988). *Neurocomputing: Foundations of research.* Cambridge, MA: MIT Press.

Andrews, G. (2001). Placebo response in depression: Bane of research, boon to therapy [Editorial]. *British Journal of Psychiatry, 178,* 192–194.

Angell, M. (2004). *The truth about the drug companies: How they deceive us and what to do about it.* New York: Random House.

Aschaffenburg, G. (1904). Experimental studies of association. In E. Kraepelin (Ed.), *Psychological works* (pp. 235–374). Leipzig: Engelmann.

Avedon, J., Meyer, F., Bolsokhoeva, N. D., Gerasimova, K. M., & Bradley, T. (1998). *The Buddha's art of healing.* New York: Rizzoli.

Bailar, J. C., III (2001). The powerful placebo and the Wizard of Oz. [letter; comment; see comments]. *New England Journal of Medicine, 344*(21), 1630–1632.

Bakal, D.A. (1999). *Minding the body: Clinical uses of somatic awareness.* New York: Guilford Press.

Balint, M. (1972). *The doctor, his patient and the illness.* New York: International Universities Press.

Bandura, A. (1997). *Self-efficacy: The exercise of control.* Cambridge, England: Cambridge University Press.

Barsky, A. J. (1992). Palpitations, cardiac awareness, and panic disorder. *American Journal of Medicine, 92,* 31–35.

Barsky, A. J., Saintfort, R., Rogers, M. P., & Borus, J. F. (2002). Nonspecific medication side effects and the nocebo phenomenon. *Journal of the American Medical Association, 287*(5), 622–627.

Bauer, P. J. (1996). What do infants recall of their lives? *American Psychologist, 51,* 29–41.

Beecher, H. K. (1955). The powerful placebo. *Journal of the American Medical Association, 159,* 1602–1606.

Benedetti, F., & Amanzio, M. (1997). The neurobiology of placebo analgesia: From endogenous opioids to cholecystokinin. *Progress in Neurobiology, 52*(2), 109–125.

Benedetti, F., Mayberg, H. S., Wager, T. D., Stohler, C. S., & Zubieta, J.-K. (2005). Neurobiological mechanisms of the placebo effect. *Journal of Neuroscience, 25,* 10390–10402.

Benedetti, F., Pollo, A., Lopiano, L., Lanotte, M., Vighetti, S., & Rainero, I. (2003). Conscious expectation and unconscious conditioning in analgesic, motor, and hormonal placebo/nocebo responses. *Journal of Neuroscience, 23*(10), 4315–4323.

Benson, H. (1996). Commentary: Self-care, the three-legged stool, and remembered wellness. *Journal of Cardiovascular Nursing, 10,* 1–3.

Benson, H., Dusk, Sherwood, J., Lam, P., Bethel, Carpenter, C. W., et al. (2006). Study of the therapeutic effects of intercessory prayer (STEP) in cardiac bypass patients: A multimember randomized trial of uncertainty and certainty of receiving intercessory prayer. *American Heart Journal, 151,* 934–942.

Benson, H., Klemchuk, H. P., & Graham, J. R. (1974). The usefulness of the relaxation response in the therapy of headache. *Headache, 14*(1), 49–52.

Benson, H., & McCallie, D. P., Jr. (1979). Angina pectoris and the placebo effect. *New England Journal of Medicine, 300*(25), 1424–1429.

Bergman, J. M., Madars, B., Johnson, S., & Spealman, R. (1989). Effects of cocaine and related drugs in non-human primates. *Journal of Pharmacology and Experimental Therapies, 251,* 150–155.

Bernard, C. (1878). *Lectures on the phenomena of life common to animals and plants.* New York: Macmillan.

Bernard, C. (1957). *Introduction to the study of experimental medicine.* New York: Dover.

Bion, W. R. (1962). *Learning from experience.* Northvale, NJ: Jason Aronson.

Bion, W. R. (1963). *Elements of psycho-analysis.* London: Heinemann.

Bliss, V. P., & Collingridge, G. L. (1993). A synaptic model of memory: Long term potentiation in the hippocampus. *Nature, 361,* 31–39.

Bodeker, G. and Kronenberg, F. (2002). A public health agenda for traditional, comlementary, and alternative medicine. *American Journal of Public Health,* 92: 1582–91.

Bodhi, B. (2000). *Discourses of the Buddha.* Sommerville, MA: Wisdom Press.

Bok, S. (1974). The ethics of giving placebos. *Scientific American, 231*(5), 17–23.

Bootzin, R. R., & Caspi, O. (2002). Explanatory mechanisms for placebo effects: Cognition, personality and social learning. In Guess et al., pp. 108–132.

Bowlby, J. (1969). *Attachment and loss.* New York: Basic Books.

Brody, H. B. (1997). Placebo response, sustained partnership, and emotional resilience in practice. *Journal of the American Board of Family Practice, 10*(1), 72–74.

Brody, H. B., & Brody, D. (2000). Placebo and health—II. Three perspectives on the placebo response: Expectancy, conditioning, and meaning. *Advances Mind-Body Medicine, 16,* 216–232.

Brown, C. (1995). *Chaos and catastrophe theories.* Thousand Oaks, CA: Sage.

Buber, M., & Smith, R. G. (1950). *I and thou.* Edinburgh: T. & T. Clark.

Calvin, W. H. (2000). *The cerebral code.* Cambridge, MA: MIT Press.

Cannon, W. (1942). Voodoo death. *American Anthropologist, 44,* 168–181.

Carey, B. (2004, October 10). Can prayers heal? Critics say research goes beyond science's reach. *The New York Times.*

Carter, C., Krener, P., Chaderjian, M., Norhtcutt, C., & Wolfe, V. (1995). Asymmetric visual-spatial attentional performance in ADHD: Evidence for a right hemispheric deficit. *Biological Psychiatry, 37,* 789–797.

Carver, C. S., & Scheir, M. F. (1998). *Self regulation of behavior.* Cambridge, MA: Cambridge University Press.

Cassells, E. J. (2004). *The nature of suffering.* Oxford: Oxford University Press.

Cobb, L., Thomas, G. I., Dillard, D.H., Merendino, K. A., & Bruce, R. A. (1959). An evaluation of internal mammary artery ligation by a double blind technique. *New England Journal of Medicine, 260*(22), 1115–1118.

Coan, J. A., Schaefer, H. S., & Davidson, R. J. (2006). Lending a hand. *Psychological Science, 17,* 1032–1039.

Cohen, B. J. (2003). *Theory and practice of psychiatry.* Oxford: Oxford University Press.

Cohen, J., & Servan-Schreiber, D. (1993). A theory of dopamine function and its role in the cognitive defects of schizophrenia. *Schizophrenia Bulletin, 19,* 85–104.

Coogan, M. D. (Ed.). (2001). *New Oxford annotated bible.* Oxford: Oxford University Press.

Cousins, N. (1995). *Anatomy of an illness.* New York: Norton.

Craig, A. (2002). How do you feel? Interoception: The sense of the physiologic condition of the body. *Nature Neuroscience, 3,* 655–666.

Csikszentmihalyi, M. (1990). *The psychology of optimal experience.* New York: Harper.

Damasio, A. (1994). *Descartes' error: Emotion, reason, and the human brain.* New York: Putnam.

Dantzer, R., Bluthe, R.-M., Laye, S., Bret-Dibat, J.-L., Panet, P., & Kelley, K. (1998). Cytokines and sickness behavior. *Annals of New York Academy of Sciences, 840,* 586–590.

Davis, C. E. (2002). Regression to the mean or placebo effect? In Guess et al., pp. 158–166.

Dawkins, R. (1990). *The selfish gene.* Oxford: Oxford University Press.

De la Fuente-Fernandez, R., Ruth, T. J., Sossi, V., Schulzer, M., Calne, D. B., & Stoessl, A. J. (2001). Expectation and dopamine release: Mechanism of the placebo effect in Parkinson's disease. *Science, 293*(5532), 1164–1166.

De la Fuente-Fernandez, R., & Stoessl, A. J. (2002). The biochemical basis of reward. *Evaluation and the Health Professions, 25,* 387–398.

Dickie, M. (2003). *Magic and magicians in the Greco-Roman world.* London: Routledge.

Dimond, E. G., Kittle, C. F., & Crockett, J. E. (1960). Comparison of internal mammary artery ligation and sham operation for angina pectoris. *American Journal of Cardiology, 5*(4), 483–486.

Doran, T. F., DeAngelis, C., Baumgardner, R., & Mellits, E. D. (1989). Acetaminophen: More harm than good? *Journal of Pediatrics, 114,* 1277–1282.

Eagle, M. (1987). *Recent developments in Attachment theory and psychoanalysis: A critical analysis.* Cambridge: Harvard University Press.

Edelman, G. (1989). *The remembered present.* New York: Basic Books.

Edelman, G. (2003). Naturalizing consciousness: A theoretical framework. *Proceedings of the National Academy of Sciences, 100,* 5520–5524.

Edelman, G., & Tononi, G. (2000). *A universe of consciousness.* New York: Basic Books.

Edelman, G. M. (2006). *Second nature: Brain science and human nature*. New Haven, CT: Yale University Press.

Edelstein, E., & Edelstein, L. (1945). *Asclepius: Collection and interpretation of the testimonies*. Baltimore: Johns Hopkins Press.

Eisenberg, D. M., Davis, R. B., Ettner, S. L., Appel, S., Wilkey, S., Van Rompay, M., et al. (1998). Trends of alternative medicine used in the United States, 1990–1997: Results of a follow-up national survey. *Journal of the American Medical Association, 280*(18), 1569–1575.

Eliade, M. (1964). *Shamanism*. Princeton, NJ: Bollingen Press.

Epstein, W.M. (1995). *The illusion of psychotherapy*. Piscataway, NJ: Transaction Publishers.

Erdman, E., & Stover, D. (2000). *Beyond a world divided*. New York: Authors Choice Press.

Ernst, E., & Resch, K. L. (1995). Concept of true and perceived placebo effects. *British Medical Journal, 311*, 551–553.

Evans, D. (2004). *Placebo*. Oxford: Oxford University Press.

FDA (2005). Alert for health care professionals. http://www.fda.gov/cder/drug/infopage/gefiitinib/default.htm.

Ferris, P. (1998). *Dr. Freud: A life*. Berkeley, CA: Counterpoint Press.

Folsom, D., Hawthorne, W., Lindamer, L., Gilmer, T., Bailey, A., Golshan, S., et al. (2005). Prevalence and risk factors for homelessness and utilization of mental health services among 10,340 patients with serious mental illness in a large public mental health system. *American Journal of Psychiatry, 162*, 370–376.

Fonagy, P. (2001). *Attachment theory and psychoanalysis*. New York: Other Press.

Fordham, M. (1974). Defences of the self. *Journal of Analytic Psychology, 19*, 192–199.

Freeman, E. W., & Rickels, K. (1999). Characteristics of placebo responses in medical treatment of premenstrual syndrome. *American Journal of Psychiatry, 159*(9), 1403–1408.

Freud, S. (1914a). On narcissism. In J. Strachey (Ed.), *The standard edition of the complete psychological works of Sigmund Freud*. (Vol. 14, pp. 67–104). London: Hogarth Press. 1991.

Freud, S. (1914b). *Remembering, repeating, and working through. In J. Strachey (Ed.), The standard edition of the complete psychological works of Sigmund Freud.* (Vol. 12, pp. 145–156) London: Hogarth Press. 1991.

Freud, S. (1923). Ego and the id. In J. Strachey (Ed.), *The standard edition of the complete psychological works of Sigmund Freud.* (Vol. 19, pp. 1–62). London: Hogarth Press. 1991.

Freud, S. (1936). New outline of psychoanalysis. In J. Strachey (Ed.), *The standard edition of the complete psychological works of Sigmund Freud.* (Vol. 23, pp. 139–208). London: Hogarth Press. 1991.

Freud, S. (1991). *The standard edition of the complete psychological works of Sigmund Freud.* J. Strachey (Ed.), Vol. 14, pp. 67–104). London: Hogarth Press.

Galton, F. (1886). Regression towards mediocrity in hereditary stature. *Jouranl of Anthropology Institute, 15*, 246–263.

Gardner, E. L. (1992). Brain reward mechanisms. In J. Lowinson and P. Ruiz (Eds.), *Substance abuse: Clinical problems and perspectives.* Baltimore: Williams & Wilkins.

Gleich, J. (1988). *Chaos.* New York: Penguin.

Goldberger, A. L., & West, B. J. (1987). Chaos in physiology: Health or disease. In H. DFegn, A. V. Holden, & L. F. Olsen (Eds.), *Chaos in biological systems.* New York: Plenum.

Goodall, J. (1996). *My life with the chimpanzees.* New York: Aladdin.

Graves, R. (1988). *The Greek myths.* Mt. Kisco NY: Moyer Bell.

Guess, H., Kleinman, A., Kusek, J., & Engel, L. (Eds.). (2002). *The science of the placebo: Towards an interdisciplinary research agenda.* London: BMJ Publishing Group.

Harrington, A. (2002). "Seeing" the placebo effect: Historical legacies and present opportunities. In Guess et al., pp. 35–52.

Hebb, D. O. (1949). *The organization of behavior.* New York: Wiley.

Hernstein, R. (1962). Placebo effect in the rat. *Science, 138*, 677–688.

Hippocrates (1964). *The theory and practice of medicine.* New York: Citadel Press.

Hofer, M. (1984). Relationships as regulators: A psychobiological perspective on bereavement. *Psychosomatic Medicine, 46*, 183–197.

Holmes, O. W. (1860). Currents and countercurrents in medical science. *Medical Essays*. Boston: Ticknor and Fields.

Houston, W. R. (1938). Doctor himself as therapeutic agent. *Annals of Internal Medicine, 11*, 1416–1425.

Hrobjartsson, A., & Goetzsche, P. C. (2001). Is the placebo powerless? An analysis of clinical trials comparing placebo with no treatment. *New England Journal of Medicine, 344*, 1594–1602.

Hume, D. (1888). *A treatise on human nature.* Oxford: Oxford University.

Humphrey, N. (2002). Great expectations: The evolutionary psychology of faith-healing and the placebo response. In N. Humphrey (Ed.), *The mind made flesh: Essays from the frontiers of evolution and psychology* (pp. 255–285). Oxford: Oxford University Press.

Hyman, S. E., Malenka, R. C., & Nestler, E. J. (2006). Neural mechanisms of addiction: The role of reward-related learning and memory. *Annual Review of Neuroscience, 29*, 565–598.

Iacobini, M., Molnar-Szakacs, I., Gallese, V., Buccino, G., Mazziotta, J. C., & Rizzolotti, G. (2005). Grasping the intentions of others with one's own mirror neuron system. *Plos Biology 3*, e79.

Jackson, S.W. (1999). Care of the psyche: A history of psychological healing. New Haven, CT: Yale University Press.

Jacobi, J. (1959). *Complex, archetype, symbol.* Princeton, NJ: Princeton University Press.

James W. (1987). Writings 1902–1910, New York: Library of America.

Jerne, N. (1996). *A portrait of the immune system.* London: World Scientific Publication.

Jung, C. (1967). The structure and dynamics of the psyche. *Collected works of C. G. Jung* (vol. 8). Princeton, NJ: Princeton University Press.

Jung, C. G. (Ed.). (1981). In H. Read, M. Fordham, G. Adler, & W. McGuire (Eds.). *Experimental researches (Collected works of C. G. Jung)* Vol. 2. Princeton, NJ: Bollingen Press.

Kandel, E., Schwartz, J. H., & Fesell, T. M. (1991). *Principles of neural science.* New York: Elsevier.

Kaptchuk, T., Edwards, R., & Eisenberg, D. (1996). Complementary medicine: Efficacy beyond the placebo effect. In E. Ernst (Ed.), *Complementary medicine: An objective appraisal* (pp. 42–70). Butterworth-Heinemann.

Katz, J. (1984). *The silent world of doctor and patient.* Baltimore: Johns Hopkins University Press.

Kienle, G., & Kiene, H. (1997). The powerful placebo response: Fact or fiction? *Journal of Clinical Epidemiology, 50,* 1311–1318.

Kirsch, I., & Weixel, L. (1988). Double blind versus deceptive administration of placebo. *Biomedical Therapeutics, 16,* 242–246.

Klein, M. (1986). *The selected Melanie Klein.* London: Hogarth Press.

Kleinman, A. (1988). *Rethinking psychiatry.* New York: Free Press.

Klopfer, B. (1957). Psychological variables in human cancer. *Journal of Projective Techniques, 21,* 221–340.

Kosslyn, S. M., & Koenig, O. (1992). *Wet minds: The new cognitive neuroscience.* New York: Free Press.

Kradin, R. (1997). The psychosomatic symptom and the self. *Journal of Analytical Psychology, 42,* 405–422.

Kradin, R. (2004a). The placebo response complex. *Journal of Analytical Psychology, 49,* 617–634.

Kradin, R. (2004b). The placebo response: Its putative role as a functional salutogenic mechanism of the central nervous system. *Perspectives in Biology and Medicine, 47*(3), 328–338.

Kradin, R. (2006). *The herald dream.* London: Karnac.

Kradin, R., & Benson, H. (2000). Stress, the relaxation response and immunity. *Modern Aspects of Immunobiology, 1,* 110–113.

Kradin, R. L. (2004). The placebo response complex. *Journal of Analytical Psychology, 50,* 18–29.

Kradin, R. L., Kurnick, J. T., Lazarus, D., Dubinett, S., Pinto, C. E., Gifford, J., et al. (1989). Tumor-infiltrating lymphocyes and interleukin-2 in the treatment of patients with advanced cancer. *Lancet, 1,* 577–580.

Kristiansen, I.S. and Mooney, G.H. (2004). *Evidence-based medicine: In its place.* New York: Routledge.

Kumin, I. (1996). *Preobject relatedness.* New York: Guilford Press.

Kuhn, T.S. (1970). *The structure of scientific revolution*. New York: Books on Demand.

Lanza, F., Goff, J., Scowcroft, C., Jennings, D., & Greski-Rose, P. (1994). Double-blind comparison of lansoprazole, ranitidine, and placebo in the treatment of acute duodenal ulcer. *American Journal of Gastroenterology, 8*, 1191–1200.

Law, J. (2006). *Big pharma*. New York: Carroll & Graff.

Leuchter, A. F., Cook, I. A., Witte, E. A., Morgan, M., & Abrams, M. (2002). Changes in brain function of depressed subjects during treatment with placebo. *American Journal of Psychiatry, 159*, 122–129.

Levine, J., Gordon, C., & Fields, H. L. (1978). The mechanism of placebo analgesia. *Lancet, 2*, 654–657.

Levine, R. J. (2002). Placebo controls in clinical trials of new therapies for conditions for which there are known effective treatments. In Guess et al., pp. 264–280.

Ley, R. (1995). Highlights of the 13th International Symposium on Respiratory Psychophysiology. *Applied Psychophysiology and Biofeedback, 20*, 369–379.

Lilford, R. J., & Braunholtz, D. A. (2001). Letter to Editor. *New England Journal of Medicine, 345*, 17.

Lin, C., Albertsen, G. A., Schilling, L. M., Cyran, E. M., Anderson, S. N., Ware, L., et al. (2001). Is patients' perception of time spent with a physician a determinant of ambulatory patient satisfaction? *Archives of Internal Medicine, 161*, 1437–1442.

Linde, K., & Clausis, N. (1997). Are the clinical effects of homeopathy placebo effects? A meta-anlaysis of placebo-controlled trials. *Lancet, 350*, 834–843.

Longo, D. L., Duffy, P. L., Kopp, W. C., Heyes, M. P., Alvord, W. G., Sharfman, W. H., et al. (1999). Conditioned immune response to inteferon-gamma in humans. *Clinical Immunology, 90*, 173–181.

Luborsky, L., Singer, B., & Luborsky, L. (1975). Comparative studies of psychotherapy: Is it true that "everyone has won and all must have prizes." *Archives of General Psychiatry, 32*, 995–1007.

Lynch, R., Bell, D., Sordella, R., Gurubhgavatula, S., Okimoto, R.A., Brannion, B. W. et al. Activating mutations in the epidermal growth factor receptor underlying responsiveness of non-small-cell lung cancer, (2004). *New England Journal of Medicine, 350*, 2129–2139.

Lyons-Ruth, K. (2001). *The early relational context of dissociation.* Paper presented at the First Research Symposium, American Psychoanalytic Association.

Maier, S. F., & Watkins, L. R. (1998). Cytokines for psychologists: Implications of bidirectional immune to brain communication for understanding behavior, mood, cognition. *Psychological Review, 105*, 83–107.

Main, M. (1995). Attachment: Overview with implications for clinical work. In S. C. Goldberg, R. Muir, & J. Kerr (Eds.), *Attachment theory: Social, developmental, and Clinical Perspectives.* Hillsdale, NJ: Analytic Press.

Majno, G. (1975). *The healing hand.* Cambridge, MA: Harvard University Press.

Masson, J. M., & McCarthy, S. (1995). *When elephants weep: The emotional lives of animals* New York: Wheeler Publishing.

Mavissakalian, M., Jones, B., & Olson, S. (1990). Absence of placebo response in obsessive-compulsive disorder. *Journal of Nervous and Mental Disease, 178*, 268–270.

Mayberg, H. S., Silva, J. A., Brannan, S. K., Tekell, J. L., Mahurin, R. K., McGinnis, S., et al. (2002). The functional neuroanatomy of the placebo response. *American Journal of Psychiatry, 159*, 728–737.

McNally, R. J., Amir, N., Louro, C. E., Lukach, B. M., Reimann, B. C., & Calamari, J. E. (1994). Cognitive processing of idiographic emotional information in panic disorder. *Behaviour Research and Therapy, 32*, 119–122.

McNally, R. J., Kaspi, S. P., & Riemann, B. C. (1990). Selective processing of threat cues in post-traumatic stress disorder. *Journal of Abnormal Psychology, 99*, 407–412.

McRae, C., Cherin, E., Yamazaki, T. G., Diem, G., Vo, A. H., Russell, D., et al. (2004). Effects of perceived treatment on quality of life and medical outcomes in a double-blind placebo surgery trial. *Archives of General Psychiatry, 61*(4), 412–420.

Meir, C. (1968). *Ancient incubation and modern psychotherapy.* Evanston, IL: Northwest University Press.

Meissner, W. W. (1996). *The therapeutic alliance.* New Haven, CT: Yale University Press.

Midgley, M. (2004). *The myths we live by.* London: Routledge.

Moerman, D. (2002). *Meaning, medicine, and the placebo effect.* Cambridge, England: Cambridge University Press.

Moerman, D. E. (2002a). Explanatory mechanisms for placebo effects: Cultural influences and the meaning response. In Guess et al., pp. 77–107.

Montgomery, G., & Kirsch, I. (1996). Mechanisms of placebo pain reduction: An empirical investigation. *Psychological Science, 7,* 174–176.

Moore, R. A., Edwards, J. E., & McQuay, H. J. (2002). Sildenafil (Viagra) for male erectile dysfunction: A meta-analysis of clinical trial reports. *BMC Urology, 2*(1), 6.

Moseley, J. B., O'Malley, K., Petersen, N. J., Menke, T. J., Brody, B. A., Kuykendall, D. H., et al. (2002). A controlled trial of arthroscopic surgery for osteoarthritis of the knee. *New England Journal of Medicine, 347,* 81–88.

Nelson, C. A., & Carver, L. J. (1998). The effects of stress and trauma on brain and memory: A view from developmental cognitive neuroscience. *Development and Psychopathology, 10,* 793–810.

Nesse, R. M., & Williams, G. C. (1996). *Why we get sick?* New York: Vintage Press.

O'Brien, E. (1999). White coat hypertension: How should it be diagnosed? *Journal of Human Hypertension, 13*(12), 801–802.

Osler, W. (1921). *The evolution of modern medicine.* New Haven, CT: Yale University Press.

Ozols, J. (2004, November 14). Doctors don't agree on risk. *Newsweek.*

Patterson, K. (2002, January 22). A visible effect: Placebo's impact in brain surprises researchers studying depression. *Dallas Morning News.*

Pepper, O. (1945). A note on the placebo. *American Journal of Pharmacology, 117,* 409–412.

Plato. (1902) *The dialogues of Plato.* New York: Charles Scribner's Sons.

Popper, K. (1972). *Objective knowledge: An evolutionary approach.* Oxford: Oxford University Press.

Porter, R. (1989). *Health for sale: Quackery in England, 1660–1850.* Manchester, England: Manchester University Press.

Porter, R. (1997). *The greatest benefit to mankind.* New York: W.W. Norton.

Porter, R. (2002). *Blood and guts.* New York: W.W. Norton and Co.

Preuss, J. (1978). *Biblical and Talmudic medicine.* Northvale: Jason Aronson.

Price, D. D., & Soerensen, L. V. (2002). Endogenous opioid and non-opioid pathways as mediators of placebo analgesia. In Guess et al., pp. 183–206.

Proust, M. (1993). *In search of lost time.* New York: Modern Library.

Quality Assurance Project (1983). Treatment outline for depressive disorders. *Australian and New Zealand Journal of Psychiatry, 17,* 129–146.

Reidenberg, M. M., & Lowenthal, D. T. (1968). Adverse nondrug reactions. *New England Journal of Medicine, 279*(13), 678–679.

Reynolds, D. (1969). Surgery in the rat during electrical analgesia induced by focal brain stimulation. *Science, 164,* 444–445.

Richardson, D., & Akil, H. (1973). Pain reduction by electrical brain stimulation in man, Part I: Acute administration in periaqueductal and periventricular sites. *Journal of Neurosurgery, 47,* 78–183.

Rizzolati, G., & Craighero, L. (2004). The mirror neuron system. *Annual Review of Neuroscience 27,* 169–192.

Robinson, D. (1995). *An intellectual history of psychology.* Madison: University of Wisconsin.

Rossi, E. (1992). *Mind body therapy: Methods of ideodynamic healing in hypnotherapy.* New York: Norton.

Rotenberg, V. (1995). Right hemisphere insufficiency and illness in the context of search activity concept. *Dynamic Psychiatry, 150,* 54–63.

Rothman, K. J., & Michels, K. B. (2002). When is it appropriate to use a placebo arm in a trial? In Guess et al., pp. 227–235.

Rueckl, J., Cave, K., & Kosslyn, S. M. (1989). Why are what and where processed by separate cortical systems? *Journal of Cognitive Neuroscience, 1,* 171–186.

Sandler, J., & Sandler, A-.M. (1998). *Internal objects revisited.* London: Karnac Books.

Sangal, R. B., & Sangal, J. M. (2003). What is a significant response in drug studies of attention-deficit/hyperactivity disorder: statistical significance is necessary, but is it sufficient? *Psychopharmacology Bulletin, 37*(2), 50–58.

Sapirstein, G., & Kirsch, I. (1998). Listening to Prozac but hearing placebo? A meta-analysis of the placebo effect of antidepressant medication. *Prevention and Treatment, 1,* 3–11.

Schopenhauer, A. (1995). *On the basis of morality.* Providence, RI: Berghan Books.

Schore, A. (1999). *Affect regulation and the origin of the self.* Mahwah, NJ: Lawrence Erlbaum.

Schore, A. (2003). *Affect dysregulation and disorders of the self.* New York: W.W. Norton & Co.

Shapiro, A. K., & Shapiro, E. (1997). *The powerful placebo: From ancient priest to modern physician.* Baltimore: Johns Hopkins University Press.

Shetty, N., Friedman, J. H., Kieburtz, K., Marshall, F. J., & Oakes, D. (1999). The placebo response in Parkinson's disease. Parkinson Study Group. *Clinical Neuropharmacology, 22*(4), 207–212.

Shorter, E. (1985). *Bedside manners.* New York: Simon & Schuster.

Shorter, E. (1993). *From paralysis to fatigue: A history of psychosomatic disease in the modern era.* New York: Free Press.

Siegel, D. J. (1999). *The developing mind.* New York: Guilford Press.

Sifneos, P. (1996). Alexithymia: Past and present. *American Journal of Psychiatry, 22,* 255–262.

Smith, D. F. (2002). Functional salutogenic mechanisms of the brain. *Perspectives in Biology and Medicine, 45,* 319–329.

Smith, M. (1978). *Jesus the magician.* Berkley, CA: Seastone.

Smith, M. L., Glass, G. V., & Miller, T. J. (1980). *The benefits of psychotherapy.* Baltimore: Johns Hopkins University Press.

Spillmann, L., & Werner, J. S. (1990). *Visual perception: The neurophsyiologic foundations.* San Diego: Academic Press.

Spitzer, M. (1999). *The mind within the net.* Cambridge, MA: MIT Press.

Stern, D. N. (1985). *The interpersonal world of the infant.* New York: Basic Books.

Sternberg, E. (2001). *The balance within.* New York: W.H. Freeman.

Stevens, S., Hynan, M., & Allen, M. (2000). A meta-analysis of common factor and specific treatment effects across the outcome domains of the phase model of psychotherapy. *Scientific Practice, 7,* 273–290.

Takagi, H., Doi, T., & Akaiake, A. (1976). Microinjection of morphine into the medial part of the bulbar reticular formation in rabbit and rat. In H. Kosterlitz (Ed.), *Opiates and endogenous opiod peptides:* Royston. Amsterdam: Elsevier.

Taylor, J. (1660). *Doctor dubitandum or the rule of conscience.* London.

Temkin, O. (1995) *Hippocrates in a World of pagans and Christians.* Baltimore: Johns Hopkins Universtiy Press, 234.

Thomas, K. B. (1987). Medical consultations: Is there any point in being positive? *British Medical Journal, 133,* 455–463.

Thomas, K. B. (1994). The placebo in general practice. *Lancet, 244,* 1066–1077.

Thompson, W. G. (2005). *Placebo effect and health: Combining science with compassionate care.* Amherst, MA: Prometheus Books.

Toates, F. (1998). The interaction of cognitive and stimulus response processes in the control of behavior. *Neuroscience and Behavioral Reviews, 22,* 59–83.

Uhlenhuth, E., Rickels, K., Fisher, S., Park, C., Lipman, S., & Mock, J. (1966). Drug, doctors verbal attitude, and clinic setting in symptomatic response to pharmacotherapy. *Psychopharmacology, 9,* 392–418.

Waitzkin, H., & Stoeckle, J. (1972). The communication of information about illness: clinical, sociological, and methodological considerations. *Advances in Psychosomatic Medicine, 180,* 187–188.

Wall, P. (2000). *Pain: The science of suffering.* New York: Columbia University Press.

Waterston, R. H., Lindblad-Toh, K., Virney, El, Rogers, J., Abril, J.F., Agarwal, P. (2002). Initial sequencing and comparative analysis of the murine genome. *Nature, 420,* 520–562.

Watkins, A., & Lewith, G. (1997). Mind–body medicine: Its popularity and perception. In A. Watkins (Ed.), *Mind–body medicine: A clinician's guide to psychoneuroimmunology* (pp. 27–40). New York: Churchill Livingston.

Watkins, A. D. (1995). Perceptions, emotions and immunity: An integrated homeostatic network. *Quarterly Journal of Medicine, 88*(4), 283–294.

Watkins, L., & Mayer, D. (1982). Involvement of the spinal opioid systems in footshock induced analgesia. *Brain Research, 242,* 309–316.

Winnicott, D. (1959). The fate of the transitional object. In *Psychoanalytic explorations.* Cambridge, MA: Harvard University Press.

Winnicott, D. (1960). *The maturational process and the facilitating environment.* New York: International Universities Press.

Wolf, S., & Pinsky, R. H. (1954). Effects of placebo administration and occurrence of toxic reactions. *Journal of the American Medical Association,* Declaration of Helsinki, 155: 339–341.

World Medical Association (2000). *Ethical principles for medical research involving human subjects.* Helsinki.

Zimbroff, D. L. (2001). Placebo response in antidepressant trials. *British Journal of Psychiatry, 178,* 573–574.

Index